justinguitar
Beginner's Songbook

PERFORMED				
LEARNED				
STARTED		**Introduction**		4
		Stage 1		6
☐☐☐		Three Little Birds	Bob Marley & The Wailers	8
☐☐☐		Feelin' Alright	Traffic	10
☐☐☐		Hound Dog	Elvis Presley	12
☐☐☐		Walk Of Life	Dire Straits	14
☐☐☐		I Walk The Line	Johnny Cash	16
☐☐☐		The Gambler	Kenny Rogers	18
☐☐☐		That's All Right	Elvis Presley	20
☐☐☐		Love Me Do	The Beatles	22
☐☐☐		How Bizarre	OMC	24
☐☐☐		Common People	Pulp	26
		Stage 2		28
☐☐☐		A Girl Like You	Edwyn Collins	30
☐☐☐		Louie Louie	The Kingsmen	32
☐☐☐		I'd Rather Go Blind	Etta James	34
☐☐☐		Natural Mystic	Bob Marley & The Wailers	36
☐☐☐		St. James Infirmary Blues	Traditional	38
☐☐☐		All Your Love (I Miss Loving)	John Mayall & The Bluesbreakers	40
☐☐☐		Twist And Shout	The Beatles	42
☐☐☐		Peggy Sue	Buddy Holly	44
☐☐☐		Lay Down Sally	Eric Clapton	46
☐☐☐		Wild Thing	The Troggs	48

continued...

Visit Hal Leonard Online at
www.halleonard.com

PERFORMED
LEARNED
STARTED

Stage 3 — 50

- ☐☐☐ Hey Joe — The Jimi Hendrix Experience — 52
- ☐☐☐ Mad World — Michael Andrews feat. Gary Jules — 54
- ☐☐☐ Hey Ya! — Outkast — 56
- ☐☐☐ Brown Eyed Girl — Van Morrison — 58
- ☐☐☐ Yellow Submarine — The Beatles — 60
- ☐☐☐ Somebody To Love — Jefferson Airplane — 62
- ☐☐☐ How To Save A Life — The Fray — 64
- ☐☐☐ What's Up? — 4 Non Blondes — 66
- ☐☐☐ This Year's Love — David Gray — 68
- ☐☐☐ Working Class Hero — John Lennon — 70

Stage 4 — 72

- ☐☐☐ Killing Me Softly With His Song — Roberta Flack — 74
- ☐☐☐ (Sittin' On) The Dock Of The Bay — Otis Redding — 76
- ☐☐☐ …Baby One More Time — Britney Spears — 78
- ☐☐☐ Save Tonight — Eagle-Eye Cherry — 80
- ☐☐☐ Celebrity — Brad Paisley — 82
- ☐☐☐ Back To December — Taylor Swift — 84
- ☐☐☐ Black — Pearl Jam — 86
- ☐☐☐ Little Lion Man — Mumford & Sons — 88
- ☐☐☐ Live Forever — Oasis — 90
- ☐☐☐ I Want To Hold Your Hand — The Beatles — 92

Stage 5 — 94

- ☐☐☐ Before You Accuse Me (Take A Look At Yourself) — Eric Clapton — 96
- ☐☐☐ Folsom Prison Blues — Johnny Cash — 98
- ☐☐☐ Sweet Little Angel — B.B. King — 100
- ☐☐☐ Crossroads — Robert Johnson — 102
- ☐☐☐ Evil (Is Going On) — Howlin' Wolf — 104
- ☐☐☐ Mary Had A Little Lamb — Stevie Ray Vaughan — 106
- ☐☐☐ Going Down Slow — Jimmy Witherspoon — 108
- ☐☐☐ I Saw Her Standing There — The Beatles — 110
- ☐☐☐ Mrs Robinson — Simon & Garfunkel — 112
- ☐☐☐ That'll Be The Day — Buddy Holly — 114

Stage 6 — 116

- ☐☐☐ Please Forgive Me — David Gray — 118
- ☐☐☐ I'm A Believer — The Monkees — 120
- ☐☐☐ Dakota — Stereophonics — 122
- ☐☐☐ No Woman, No Cry — Bob Marley & The Wailers — 124
- ☐☐☐ Can't Help Falling In Love — Elvis Presley — 126
- ☐☐☐ Pink Bullets — The Shins — 128
- ☐☐☐ The Thrill Is Gone — B.B. King — 130
- ☐☐☐ Mr. Jones — Counting Crows — 132
- ☐☐☐ The Drugs Don't Work — The Verve — 134
- ☐☐☐ House Of The Rising Sun — Traditional — 136

STARTED LEARNED PERFORMED

Stage 7 — 138
- ☐☐☐ Summer Of '69 — Bryan Adams — 140
- ☐☐☐ Wanted Dead Or Alive — Bon Jovi — 142
- ☐☐☐ Lucky Man — The Verve — 144
- ☐☐☐ California Dreamin' — The Mamas & The Papas — 146
- ☐☐☐ Don't You (Forget About Me) — Simple Minds — 148
- ☐☐☐ You Really Got Me — The Kinks — 150
- ☐☐☐ Have A Nice Day — Stereophonics — 152
- ☐☐☐ Love Is All Around — The Troggs — 154
- ☐☐☐ Down Under — Men At Work — 156
- ☐☐☐ Weather With You — Crowded House — 158

Stage 8 — 160
- ☐☐☐ Hallelujah — Leonard Cohen — 162
- ☐☐☐ Fast Car — Tracy Chapman — 164
- ☐☐☐ Fields Of Gold — Sting — 166
- ☐☐☐ Vincent — Don McLean — 168
- ☐☐☐ Wonderwall — Oasis — 170
- ☐☐☐ Polly — Nirvana — 172
- ☐☐☐ Molly's Chambers — Kings Of Leon — 174
- ☐☐☐ The Sound Of Silence — Simon & Garfunkel — 176
- ☐☐☐ All The Small Things — Blink-182 — 178
- ☐☐☐ Pretty Fly (For A White Guy) — The Offspring — 180

Stage 9 — 182
- ☐☐☐ Better Be Home Soon — Crowded House — 184
- ☐☐☐ Have You Ever Seen The Rain — Creedence Clearwater Revival — 186
- ☐☐☐ Wherever You Will Go — The Calling — 188
- ☐☐☐ American Pie — Don McLean — 190
- ☐☐☐ Redemption Song — Bob Marley & The Wailers — 192
- ☐☐☐ Wonderful Tonight — Eric Clapton — 194
- ☐☐☐ The A Team — Ed Sheeran — 196
- ☐☐☐ Zombie — The Cranberries — 198
- ☐☐☐ Hand In My Pocket — Alanis Morissette — 200
- ☐☐☐ Let It Be — The Beatles — 202

Bonus Songs — 203
- ☐☐☐ You're Beautiful — James Blunt — 204
- ☐☐☐ Imagine — John Lennon — 206
- ☐☐☐ Hey, Soul Sister — Train — 208
- ☐☐☐ Wild World — Cat Stevens — 210
- ☐☐☐ Use Somebody — Kings Of Leon — 212
- ☐☐☐ Stuck In The Middle With You — Stealers Wheel — 214
- ☐☐☐ Dream Catch Me — Newton Faulkner — 216
- ☐☐☐ Substitute — The Who — 218
- ☐☐☐ Driftwood — Travis — 220
- ☐☐☐ Times Like These — Foo Fighters — 222

Credits — 224

INTRODUCTION

 Hi, Justin here. Welcome to my Beginner's Songbook!

This book is designed to be used in conjunction with my Beginner's Guitar Course, which is a series of almost 100 lessons to get you started in the right way on guitar. The course has been used by many hundreds of thousands of people all over the world, and is probably the most-used guitar method ever!

If you are stuck on a technique, or don't understand something, then your first port of call should be the Beginner's Course at the relevant stage—it is very likely you will find your answer.

I don't expect everyone will like all the songs in each level, but I'm hoping that the range of styles represented across the 100 songs in this book—from The Beatles and Bob Marley to Foo Fighters—will mean that there are several songs in each stage that you will like.

Sometimes the songs may seem a little hard for the stage they appear in, but they are there for a reason: introducing a particular skill. Bear in mind that ALL the songs in this book should be revisited a few times as you progress. Often there are strumming patterns or other techniques introduced for a song which are deliberately more advanced than the stage that song appears in; these can be looked at further down the line as you get to the later stages. Your confidence will develop as you get better playing the song with each visit.

I'd like to thank all those Facebook and Twitter fans who helped out with song ideas and the Music Sales team, especially Tom Farncombe, for his help in putting it all together and offering many useful suggestions.

Justin Sandercoe
December 2015, London

Here's what you'll see for each song!

Look out throughout the book for references to the relevant lesson in the Beginner's Course, shown by lesson code: BC-XXX etc.

Song title

If you need to use a capo to match the key of the original record, the fret to place the capo at is shown here

These tabs show you which stage of the course the song is appropriate for

The shaded bar shows the sections of the song

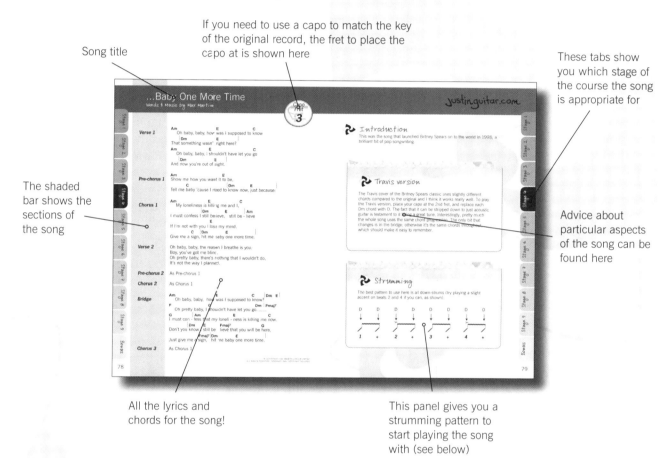

Advice about particular aspects of the song can be found here

All the lyrics and chords for the song!

This panel gives you a strumming pattern to start playing the song with (see below)

Strumming patterns

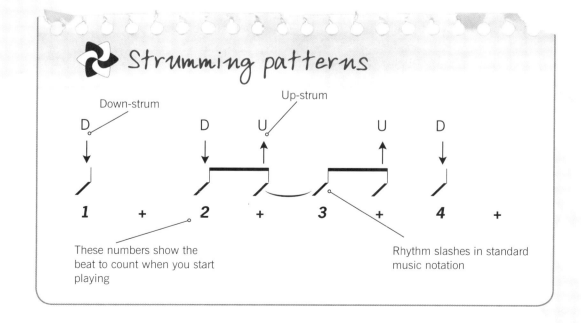

Down-strum

Up-strum

These numbers show the beat to count when you start playing

Rhythm slashes in standard music notation

STAGE 1 BC-111—BC-119

 ## Introduction

Welcome to Stage 1! At this stage you only learn three chords, and will only be playing very simple four-strums-per-bar patterns, as shown opposite. There are not a whole lot of songs (if any!) that really use this strumming throughout, so when you play these songs they might not sound exactly like the record—but they should be recognizable as the original song, and as your skills improve the songs will sound better. So, remember that you should re-visit these songs as you progress along the course.

The thing to aim for in Stage 1 is being able to keep the four-strums-per-bar even in tempo (speed) without leaving gaps between the chord changes. At first this might seem impossible—but this is the goal. If you keep working on your 'One-Minute Changes' (see opposite) and picking your chords one note at a time you will soon be able to change between chords quickly and clearly. Don't expect it to come too soon. It WILL take practice—but you WILL get there!

Many of the songs suggest using a capo, but you don't have to use one. A capo will help you play along with the original recording, which is definitely fun, and I recommend that you give this a go once you can play through a song confidently. If you're really keen on using a capo from the start then I recommend starting out by just playing the chords in open position, working on your chord changes and keeping your strumming even, bringing in the capo when you are confident with your rhythm playing and want to start working along with the original recorded versions.

It's really helpful when you're starting out to have a chord written in for every bar it is played. This concept goes a bit wrong in complex music, or when a chord only lasts half a bar, and this is probably why most sheet music books don't do this (you can always add them in yourself if that is the case). I did that as a kid and found it makes keeping your place in the song a lot easier! So, count along while you sing the words in your head and write the chord in each time you get back to '1' (the start of the bar). You can see a good example of this in 'Common People' (page 26), where one chord is played for a lot of bars.

The music in this book isn't written out using full music notation, but we have used barlines to show where some of the chord changes fall. Whenever you see a chord symbol, it almost always means that you play that chord for a full bar (four strums); where two chords are shown between barlines, it almost always means that you play each chord for two beats (two strums) each.

Two more things, about chord symbols: some of the songs—for instance, 'Love Me Do' (Page 22)— use the symbol N.C. at various points. This stands for 'no chord', and simply means that you don't play anything there! Also, sometimes you'll see a chord symbol in parentheses (e.g., 'Twist And Shout' and 'Black'). This is simply to indicate where a new section of lyrics begins during the last chord of the previous section, so that you don't play too many strums on that chord.

Stage 1 Chords

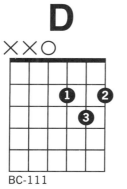
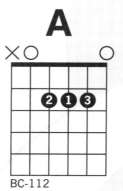
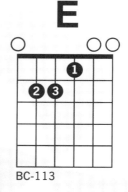

One-Minute Changes BC-115

Once you know how to play your chords the big challenge is to get your chord changes clear and fast so that you can play a song without stopping between chords. You should be able to do this well before you start trying to play strumming patterns, or your songs will always sound disjointed and kind of silly!

The trick is to focus on changing between two particular chords for one minute. Use a stopwatch, or the countdown feature on your phone, and see how many times you can change between two chords, taking care to hold each one correctly and make each one clear.

You will find this will make a HUGE difference if you stick at it! Do it every day. I see great results with this all the time with private students and I know you will see a fast improvement too! Keep a record of how times you make the change each session. You will find that being able to watch your progress will really help keep you motivated.

Strumming four-to-a-bar BC-116

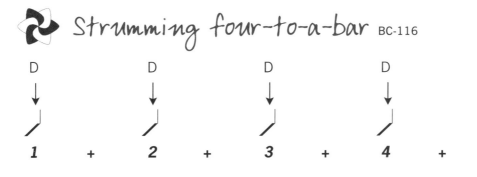

Three Little Birds
Words & Music by Bob Marley

Intro | A | A | A | A |

Chorus 1
      A   A
Don't worry about a thing,
      D   A
'Cause every little thing gonna be all right.
            A   A
Singin' don't worry about a thing,
      D   A
'Cause every little thing gonna be all right!

Verse 1
        A   E
Rise up this mornin', smiled with the risin' sun,
     A   D
Three little birds pitch by my doorstep
     A   E
Singin' sweet songs of melodies pure and true,
       D   A
Sayin', "This is my message to you-ou-ou:"

Chorus 2 As Chorus 1

Verse 2
Rise up this mornin' smiled with the risin' sun,
Three little birds pitch by my doorstep
Singin' sweet songs of melodies pure and true,
Sayin', "This is my message to you-ou-ou:"

Chorus 3 As Chorus 1 *Repeat to fade*

© COPYRIGHT 1977 BLUE MOUNTAIN MUSIC LIMITED.
ALL RIGHTS RESERVED. INTERNATIONAL COPYRIGHT SECURED.

Introduction

This reggae classic first appeared on Bob Marley's 1977 album *Exodus*. It's a perfect song to get you started on chord changes and easy four-to-a-bar strumming.

Easy Strumming and Counting

Make sure that you strum four times each time a chord is shown above the lyrics. Aim to keep the strums evenly spaced, and try not to let yourself pause between chords. If you are very new to playing then there may well be a little gap while you change, but keep trying to make each change as smooth as possible. It's fine to count along '1, 2, 3, 4' with each strum; many people find that helpful.

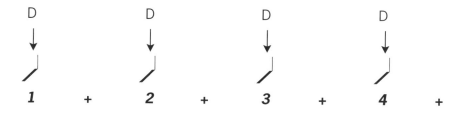

Playing the Off-Beats

Once you have progressed through Stage 4, it would be cool to come back and visit this song and play only the off-beats (the 'ands' between the beats) to give it a laid-back reggae feel. It might feel a little strange, because you count '1', then strum, count '2' and then the strum etc., but it sounds very cool! You can use either down- or up-strums between the beats in this song: up-strums are probably a little easier though and will give a more authentic reggae sound.

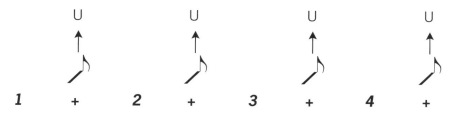

Feelin' Alright
Words & Music by Dave Mason

Capo Fret 3

Verse 1

    A   D
It seems I've got to have a change of scene,
    A   D
'Cause every night I have the strangest dreams.
    A   D
Imprisoned by the way it could have been,
    A   D
Left here on my own or so it seems.
    A   D
I've got to leave before I start to scream,
    A   D
But someone's locked the door and took the key.

Chorus 1

(D)   A   D   A   D
You feelin' alright?   I'm not feelin' too good myself.
       A   D   A   D
Well, you feelin' alright?   I'm not feelin' too good myself.

Verse 2

Well boy, you sure took me for one big ride
And even now I sit and wonder why
That when I think of you I start to cry,
I just can't waste my time, I must keep dry.
Gotta stop believin' in all your lies,
'Cause there's too much to do before I die.

Chorus 2   As Chorus 1

Verse 3

Don't get too lost in all I say,
Though at the time I really felt that way.
But that was then, now it's today,
Can't get off yet and so I'm here to stay,
Till someone comes along and takes my place
With a different name and, yes, a different face.

Chorus 3   As Chorus 1

© COPYRIGHT 1968 UNIVERSAL/ISLAND MUSIC LIMITED.
RESERVED. INTERNATIONAL COPYRIGHT SECURED.

Introduction

Traffic's 1968 hit, widely covered, showing what you can do with two chords and attitude…

Using a Capo

You can of course play this song without a capo and it will sound cool, but in a different key. You only need to use the capo if you want to play along with the original recording. Placing the capo at the 3rd fret will work for the Traffic original and also the famous version by Joe Cocker. However, other versions may require the capo at a different fret, so watch out for that!

Changing Patterns

Most songs can be played with many different strumming patterns, and part of learning to play guitar is to experiment with different ones. To begin with I suggest playing four down-strums in a bar, but as you progress then you should try using other patterns. This is a great song for that, because it has one chord per bar for the whole song. You can't ask for easier than that

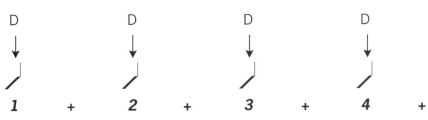

Hound Dog

Words & Music by Jerry Leiber & Mike Stoller

Capo Fret **3**

Chorus 1

N.C.   **A**   **A**   **A**   **A**
You ain't nothing but a hound dog,   crying all the time.
                          D   **D**   **A**   **A**
You ain't nothing but a hound dog,   crying all the time.
                E
Well, you ain't never caught a rabbit
        D   **A**   **A**
And you ain't no friend of mine.

Verse 1

Well they said you was high class, well that was just a lie,
Yeah they said you was high class, well that was just a lie.
Yeah, you ain't never caught a rabbit
And you ain't no friend of mine.

Chorus 2   As Chorus 1

Solo

A	A	A	A
D	D	A	A
E	D	A	A

NB: The chords for the solo are a classic 12-Bar Blues sequence (see opposite).

Verse 2   As Verse 1

Solo   12-bar blues form (as Solo 1)

Verse 3   As Verse 1

Chorus 3   As Chorus 1

© COPYRIGHT 1956 UNIVERSAL/MCA MUSIC LIMITED/CHAPPELL MORRIS LIMITED.
ALL RIGHTS RESERVED. INTERNATIONAL COPYRIGHT SECURED.

Introduction

This song is usually associated with Elvis Presley, but it's well worth checking out the original version by Big Mama Thornton (1952).

The 12-Bar Blues

The sequence of chords used in this song is very common and is known as a 12-Bar Blues. It has 12 bars (naturally) and the pattern of chords is basically always the same, though there are some variations you may come across later. After you have completed Stage 5 you might like to come back to this and use the chords A7, D7 and E7 instead of A, D and E—they will sound cool too!

Silent or Ring?

In the breaks in this song you could either let one strum ring out or mute the strings (with the outer palm of your strumming hand). Both will sound cool; give them a try and see which you prefer. There are many strumming patterns that will work for this song. Start with the basic four-strums-per-bar, and when we've looked at up-strums (Stage 3), come back and try this strumming pattern:

D   D   D   U   D

   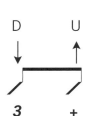 

1 +   2 +   3 +   4 +

Walk Of Life
Words & Music by Mark Knopfler

Capo Fret 7

| Intro | ‖: A | D | E | D E :‖ Play 4 times |

Verse 1
A (play for four bars)
Here comes Johnny singing oldies, goldies
Be-Bop-A-Lula, Baby What I Say
Here comes Johnny singing I Gotta Woman
Down in the tunnels, trying to make it pay

Pre-Chorus 1
D
   He got the action, he got the motion
A
   Yeah the boy can play
D
   Dedication, devotion
A
Turning all the night time into the day

Chorus 1
    |A   E
He do the song about the sweet lovin' woman
    |A   D
He do the song about the knife
    |A   E |D
He do the walk,   he do the walk of life
E
Yeah, he do the walk of life

| Link | | A | D | E | D E | |

Verse 2
Here comes Johnny and he'll tell you the story
Hand me down my walkin' shoes
Here come Johnny with the power and the glory
Backbeat the talkin' blues

Pre-Chorus 2 — As Pre-Chorus 1

Chorus 2 — As Chorus 1

| Link | ‖: A | D | E | D E :‖ |

Verse 3 — As Verse 1

Pre-Chorus 3 — As Pre-Chorus 1

Chorus 3
And after all the violence and double talk
There's just a song in all the trouble and the strife
You do the walk, you do the walk of life
You do the walk of life

| Coda | ‖: A | D | E | D E :‖ Repeat to fade |

© COPYRIGHT 1985 STRAITJACKET SONGS LIMITED.
UNIVERSAL MUSIC PUBLISHING LIMITED.
ALL RIGHTS RESERVED. INTERNATIONAL COPYRIGHT SECURED.

Introduction

From the smash-hit album *Brothers In Arms*, this rockabilly-style Dire Straits song originally featured organ and several guitars, but translates well to strumming on a single guitar.

 ## Playing with a Capo

The frets on a guitar get narrower as you move up the neck, so it can be hard to place your fingers at the right frets for the chords when you have a capo right up at the 7th fret, such as for this song. I would recommend starting without the capo to learn the chords, and then play along with the recording when you can play without stopping for chord changes and you're ready for a challenge.

 ## Verse strumming

Each verse has four bars of strumming on an A chord—we didn't have to write it out all four times, did we?

Spreads

There are parts of this song where it sounds best to play just one big strum and let it ring out. When you do this it is very important that you keep your foot tapping, or count out loud so you keep the tempo steady. If you don't have something to keep the timing even, you will most likely come in too early with the next chord. For the rest of the song you can play four down-strums per chord for now; later, add the rock 'n' roll shuffle (shown in BC-183) when you reach Stage 8.

D
↓

```
1    +    2    +    3    +    4    +
```

I Walk The Line

Words & Music by Johnny Cash

Verse 1

      E   A
I keep a close watch on this heart of mine
     E   A
I keep my eyes wide open all the time.
      D   A
I keep the ends out for the tie that binds,
               E   A
Because you're mine, I walk the line.

Verse 2

I find it very, very easy to be true
I find myself alone when each day is through
Yes I'll admit that I'm a fool for you,
Because you're mine, I walk the line.

Verse 3

As sure as night is dark and day is light,
I keep you on my mind both day and night.
And happiness I've known proves that it's right
Because you're mine, I walk the line.

Verse 4

You've got a way to keep me on your side
You give me cause for love that I can't hide.
For you I know I'd even try and turn the tide
Because you're mine, I walk the line.

Verse 5

I keep a close watch on this heart of mine,
I keep my eyes wide open all the time.
I keep the ends out for the tie that binds,
Because you're mine, I walk the line.

© COPYRIGHT 1956 HILL AND RANGE SONGS INCORPORATED/UNICHAPPELL MUSIC INCORPORATED, USA.
CARLIN MUSIC CORPORATION.
ALL RIGHTS RESERVED. INTERNATIONAL COPYRIGHT SECURED.

Introduction

The song, the movie, the man… one of *the* definitive Country songs.

Simplifications

This song has been heavily simplified so you can play it with just three chords. The original version has some key changes and we've just pulled it back so it's all in the same key. So, don't try and play this along with the recording. It really won't sound nice!

'Boom chick-a boom chick-a'

Make sure you master this song playing four-strums-per-bar before trying more advanced strumming. When you're feeling confident, you could have a go at the pattern below—Johnny Cash used this kind of strum a lot. This 'train' strumming sounds best with a heavy accent on beats 2 and 4, with the off-beats played very lightly. Think 'boom chick-a boom chick-a'.

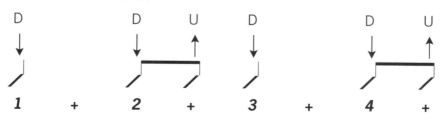

The Gambler
Words & Music by Don Schlitz

Capo Fret 6

Intro | A | D | A | D |

Verse 1
     A   A   D   A
On a warm summer's evenin' on a train bound for nowhere,
 A   A   A   E
I met up with the gambler, we were both too tired to sleep.
    A   A   D   A
So we took turns a-starin' out the window at the darkness,
    D   A   E   A
Till boredom over - took us   and he began to speak.

Verse 2
He said, "Son, I've made a life out of readin' people's faces,
Knowin' what their cards were by the way they held their eyes.
So if you don't mind my sayin', I can see you're out of aces
For a taste of your whiskey I'll give you some advice."

Verse 3
So I handed him my bottle and he drank down my last swallow,
Then he bummed a cigarette and asked me for a light.
And the night got deathly quiet and his face lost all expression
He said, "If you're gonna play the game, boy you gotta learn to play it right."

Chorus 1
          A   A   D   A
"You've got to know when to hold 'em,   know when to fold 'em,
D   A   A   E
Know when to walk away and know when to run.
    A   A   D   A
You never count your money when you're sittin' at the table,
     D   A E   A
There'll be time enough for countin'   when the dealin's done."

Verse 4
"Every gambler knows that the secret to sur - vivin'
Is knowin' what to throw away and knowin' what to keep.
'Cause every hand's a winner and every hand's a loser
And the best that you can hope for is to die in your sleep."

Verse 5
And when he finished speakin' he turned back toward the window,
Crushed out his cigarette and faded off to sleep.
And somewhere in the darkness the gambler he broke even,
But in his final words I found an ace that I could keep.

Chorus 2–4 As Chorus 1 (*Play x3; 2º* without guitar)

© COPYRIGHT 1978 CROSS KEYS PUBLISHING COMPANY INCORPORATED, USA.
SONY/ATV MUSIC PUBLISHING.
ALL RIGHTS RESERVED. INTERNATIONAL COPYRIGHT SECURED.

Introduction

Timeless card-playing advice from Kenny Rogers.

Simplifications

The original version of this song has some key changes in it, and so you can't play along all the way through with the original recording of this one. You could play along with the start of it, but you'll have to stop about three quarters of the way through (after Chorus 1). Many otherwise easy songs have something difficult about them that might prevent you playing the song at all. I always think that making the song easier, so you can actually play it, is better than nothing; when you're playing by yourself you can do it without the key changes anyway!

Counting Strums

If you find yourself struggling to know how many strums to play of each chord, then it can help to get a red pen out and write the number of strums next to the chord. You'll probably find that writing it down actually helps it stick in your memory, as well.

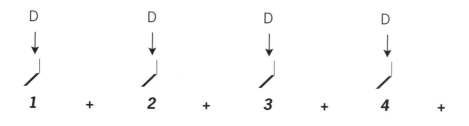

That's All Right
Words & Music by Arthur Crudup

Intro | A | A |

Verse 1
        A   A
Well, that's all right, mama, that's all right for you.
A   A
That's all right mama, just any way you do.
               D   D
Well, that's all right, that's all right.
         E   E   A
That's all right now, mama, any way you do.

Verse 2
Well Mama she done told me, Papa done told me too,
"Son, that gal you're foolin' with, she ain't no good for you."
But, that's all right, that's all right.
That's all right now mama, any way you do.

Solo | A | A | A | A |
         | D | D | E | E | A | A |

Verse 3
I'm leaving town, baby, I'm leaving town for sure.
Well, then you won't be bothered with me hanging 'round your door.
Well, that's all right, that's all right.
That's all right now mama, any way you do.

Coda
       A   A
Ah da da dee dee dee dee, dee dee dee dee,
A
Dee dee dee dee.
         D   D
I need your loving, that's all right,
         E   E   A
That's all right now mama, any way you do.

| A | A |

© COPYRIGHT 1947 (RENEWED) CRUDUP MUSIC/UNICHAPPELL MUSIC INCORPORATED, USA.
REPRODUCED BY KIND PERMISSION OF CARLIN MUSIC CORPORATION.
ALL RIGHTS RESERVED. INTERNATIONAL COPYRIGHT SECURED.

Introduction

'That's All Right' (1954) was Elvis Presley's very first single. The song is a cover version of the Arthur Crudup tune, and was recorded during a spontaneous jamming session in Sun Studios, Memphis.

Easy!

This one is a great, fun beginner song, using just A, D and E, with not too many chord changes, and it doesn't even need a capo! Because you play the first chord of the verse for four bars—that's sixteen strums if you are playing four to the bar—you'll need to develop a feeling for when each new bar starts. The best way to do that is to simply count the four beats in each bar when you practise and to slightly accent the beat 1 strum. After a while you should stop counting and just feel the four beats, but check yourself every now and then and make sure you are doing it right!

Do watch out in the Coda if you play along with the original recording because it seems the 'King' decided to give the chop to one of the four A chords that appear in all the other verses!

Strumming

The original song is pretty fast so I would recommend just playing a down-strum on each beat and keeping it really simple. If it's too fast for you, just play on beats 1 and 3. The actual pattern played on the recording is taught in Stage 7, so once you've learnt it, you should come back and apply that fancy pattern (where you pick out the bass note on beats 1 and 3) because it sounds really cool!

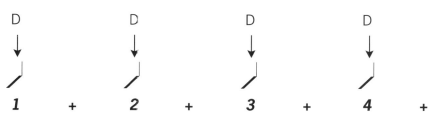

Love Me Do
Words & Music by John Lennon & Paul McCartney

Capo Fret **10**

Intro

| A | D | A | D | A | D | A | A |

Chorus 1

   A   **D**
Love, love me do,
        A   **D**
You know I love you.
      A   **D**
I'll always be true,
  D   **D**
So please____
N.C. **A**   **D** **A**   **D**
Love me do, ___ oh, love me do.

Chorus 2 As Chorus 1

Bridge

 E   **E**
Someone to love,
 D   **A**
Somebody new.
 E   **E**
Someone to love,
 D   **A**
Someone like you.

Chorus 3 As Chorus 1

Solo As Bridge chords

Chorus 4 As Chorus 1 *(Repeat to fade)*

© COPYRIGHT 1962 MPL COMMUNICATIONS LIMITED.
ALL RIGHTS RESERVED. INTERNATIONAL COPYRIGHT SECURED.

Introduction

The Beatles' first single. Three chords. The most successful group of all time. There's a lesson there…

Mute the Strings!

When you see the symbol N.C (No chord) it's a good idea to rest the edge of your strumming hand on the strings to silence the guitar. If you don't, many of the strings will keep ringing out, which isn't the idea. Remember, sometimes the silences are as important as the chords!

Placing the capo on the 10th fret (to play along with the original record) is very uncomfortable, as you're playing so far up the neck, so I recommend playing it in open position; we've changed the key of the song so you can play it with just A, D and E.

Accent the '2'

As ever, work on getting your four-to-the-bar strumming solid first, but come back to this song and try the pattern below when you've started learning about up-strums.

This pattern sounds best if you play the down-strum on beat 2 a little harder than the others. Make sure you start by getting the whole pattern right at medium volume and then try a bit more volume on the beat 2 down-strum. Experimenting with accents can add a lot of depth to your playing.

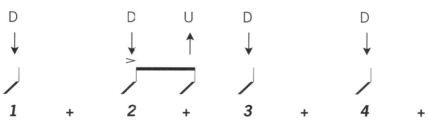

How Bizarre
Words & Music by Alan Jansson & Paul Fuemana

Capo Fret 3

Chord progression throughout:
| A   E | D |

Verse 1
Brother Pele's in the back, sweet Seena's in the front,
Cruising down the freeway in the hot, hot sun,
Suddenly red blue lights flash us from behind,
Loud voice booming, "Please step out onto the line."
Pele breathes words of comfort, Seena just hides her eyes,
Policeman taps his shades, "Is that a Chevy 69?"

Chorus 1
How bizarre, how bizarre, how bizarre.

Verse 2
Destination unknown, as we pull in for some gas,
A freshly pasted poster reveals a smile from the pack.
Elephants and acrobats, lions, snakes, monkey,
Pele speaks righteous, Sister Seena says, "Funky."

Chorus 2
As Chorus 1

Bridge 1
Ooh baby, (ooh baby),
It's making me crazy, (it's making me crazy),
Every time I look around, (look around),
Every time I look around, (every time I look around),
Every time I look around it's in my face.

Verse 3
Ringmaster steps up, says "The elephants left town,"
People jump and jive, and the clowns inch back around.
T.V. news and cameras, there's choppers in the sky,
Marines, police, reporters, ask where, for and why.
Pele yells "We're outta here," Seena says "Right on."
Make your moves and starting grooves, before they knew we were gone.
Jumped into the Chevy, headed for big lights,
Wanna know the rest? Hey, buy the rights.

Chorus 3
As Chorus 1

Bridge 2
As Bridge 1 (*Play x3*)

© COPYRIGHT 1995 UNIVERSAL MUSIC PUBLISHING LIMITED.
RESERVED. INTERNATIONAL CCPYRIGHT SECURED.

Introduction

One-hit-wonders OMC released this laid-back anthem in 1996. It still goes down a storm on Waitangi Day!

 ## BBQ Favourites

Some songs, like this one, have a chord sequence that repeats for the whole song. They are so simple that you should try to make sure you remember them right away, as you have no excuse not to! They are great ones to pull out at a BBQ or house party too because even if you are full of the 'party spirit' you should be able to get through simple songs like this!

Adding 'Ands'

The strum pattern used in this song is simple and fun. You just add in an up-strum after the 2nd and 4th down-strums. This is covered fully in Stage 3, but you could try sneaking a couple here in Stage 1. It won't hurt! The crucial thing is making sure that you keep moving your hand consistently and evenly, no matter what pattern you are strumming. This will come with practice, so don't stress if you are new to guitar and are having trouble—the vast majority of beginners really struggle with strumming!

 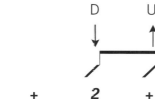  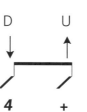

Common People

Words by Jarvis Cocker • Music by Jarvis Cocker, Nick Banks, Russell Senior, Candida Doyle & Stephen Mackey

Capo Fret 3

Verse 1

```
     A                          A
     She came from Greece, she had a thirst for knowledge,
     A                     A
     She studied sculpture at St. Martin's college,
                    E    E           E         E
That's where I     caught her eye.
     A                         A
     She told me that her dad was loaded,
     A                                      A
     I said "In that case I'll have rum and Coca Cola,"
             E        E          E              E
She said "Fine"     and then in thirty seconds time she said
       D                D
       "I want to live like common people,
       D                D
       I want to do what - ever common people do,
       A                     A
       Want to sleep with common people,
       A                   A                  E
       I want to sleep with   common people like you."
E                E                  E                  A
Well, what else could I do? I said, "I'll - I'll see what I can do."
```

Verse 2

I took her to a supermarket,
I don't know why but I had to start it somewhere, so it started there.
I said "Pretend you've got no money,"
She just laughed and said "Oh, you're so funny," I said "Yeah?
Well I can't see anyone else smiling in here,
Are you sure you want to live like common people,
You want to see whatever common people see,
You want to sleep with common people,
You want to sleep with common people like me?"
But she didn't understand, she just smiled and held my hand.

Verse 3

Rent a flat above a shop, cut your hair and get a job,
Smoke some fags and play some pool, pretend you never went to school,
But still you'll never get it right 'cause when you're laid in bed at night
Watching 'roaches climb the wall,
If you called your dad he could stop it all, yeah.
You'll never live like common people,
You'll never do whatever common people do.
You'll never fail like common people,
You'll never watch your life slide out of view,
And then dance and drink and screw
Because there's nothing else to do.

Instrumental

```
||: A   | A   | A   | A   |
|  E   | E   | E   | E   :||
```

© COPYRIGHT 1994 ISLAND MUSIC LIMITED.
UNIVERSAL/ISLAND MUSIC LIMITED.
ALL RIGHTS RESERVED. INTERNATIONAL COPYRIGHT SECURED.

Verse 4
Sing along with the common people,
Sing along and it might just get you through.
Laugh along with the common people,
Laugh along even though they're laughing at you,
And the stupid things that you do,
Because you think that poor is cool.

Verse 5
Like a dog lying in the corner,
They will bite you and never warn you,
Look out, they'll tear your insides out,
'Cause everybody hates a tourist,
Especially one who thinks it's all such a laugh,
And the chip stains and grease will come out in the bath.
You will never understand how it feels to live your life
With no meaning or control and with nowhere left to go.
You are amazed that they exist,
And they burn so bright whilst you can only wonder why.

Verse 6 As Verse 3

Outro | A | A | A | A |

(A)
‖: Want to live with common people like you… :‖

 ## Introduction

Pulp's breakthrough in 1995, and a great three-chord sing-along. A song which works brilliantly for solo guitar despite the synthy production on the original.

Pumping '8s'

The strumming in this song is really simple, but this pattern isn't actually covered in Stage 1—but because it sounds so cool for this song I'm going to show you now. The pattern uses down-strums on each beat and every 'and'. This is often called 'Pumping 8s' and is used a lot in rock, punk and other high energy music. Try it out, maybe making the verses quiet and the choruses loud to keep it interesting.

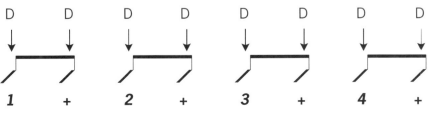

STAGE 2

Introduction

In Stage 2 we introduce three minor chords for you to learn.

I believe that it will take you some time to get your rhythm solid, so again, that is the thing you should really focus your attention on. Try to play some songs using a metronome while tapping your foot if you can (see BC-125 and BC-126).

Developing a strong sense of rhythm is one of the most important (and oh-so-often-forgotten) skills for any guitar player and the best ways to develop it are by practising tapping your foot with the beat, and using a metronome. I would also highly recommend getting into the habit of tapping your foot along every time you hear music—make it something that happens naturally and it will always be there to help you!

Don't forget to keep revising some of the songs from the previous stage too. You will find it easier to apply your foot-tapping or metronome work with a song that you have already been working on, rather than applying it to a new one straight away.

To see the best improvement, you want a mix of some songs that you find easy—to build your confidence with—and some songs which push your technique and chord changes. It can be tricky to find the right balance. The easiest way to find it is to see what you enjoy! It's got to be fun; if you are spending too much time getting frustrated by harder songs, go back and consolidate your skills on the previous tunes before having a go at the new ones.

Be aware that most of the songs here have alternate strumming patterns shown, but if you are just starting Stage 2 you should keep to playing four-strums-per-bar and tapping your foot. I have included more fancy patterns so as you develop your skills you can return to the song and make it sound cooler, but it's very important that you just stick to the easy strumming while you develop your chord changes. I know it's hard, but be patient, and you'll get there faster.

Stage 2 Chords

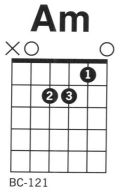
Am
BC-121

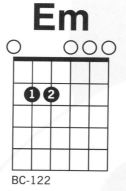
Em
BC-122

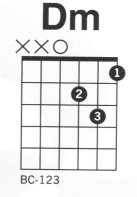
Dm
BC-123

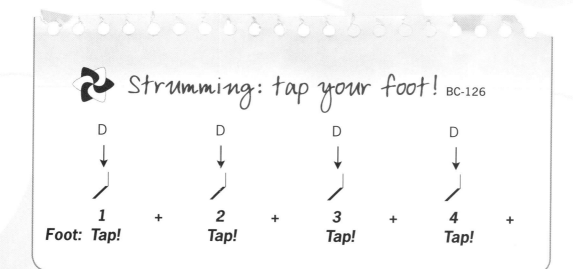

Strumming: tap your foot! BC-126

A Girl Like You

Words & Music by Edwyn Collins

Capo Fret 3

| Intro | \| Am   \| Dm Em \| Am   \| Dm Am \|
| | \| Am   \| Dm Em \| Am   \| Dm Am \|

Verse 1

      Am |Dm   Em|Am |Dm Am|
I've never known a girl like you be - fore,
      Am |Dm   Em|Am |Dm Am|
Now just like in a song from days of yore.
Am |Dm   Em|Am |Dm Am|
Here you come a-knocking, knocking on my door,
      Am |Dm   Am|Am |Dm Am|
And I've never met a girl like you be - fore.

Guitar riff 1   As Intro Chords

Verse 2

You give me just a taste so I want more,
Now my hands are bleeding and my knees are raw,
'Cause now you've got me crawling, crawling on the floor,
An' I've never known a girl like you before.

Guitar riff 2   As Intro Chords

Verse 3

Am |Dm   Em|
You've made me acknowledge the devil in me,
Am |Dm   Em|
I hope to God I'm talking meta - phorical - ly,
Am |Dm   Em |
I hope that I'm taking alle - gorical - ly,
Am |Dm   Em |
Know that I'm talking 'bout the way I feel.
      Am |Dm   Am|Am |Dm Am|
An' I've never known a girl like you be - fore,
Am |Dm Em |
Never, never, never, never,
Am |Dm   Am |
Never known a girl like you be - fore.

Guitar solo   As Intro Chords

Outro

Am |Dm   Em | Am |Dm   Em |
  This old town's changed so much,   don't feel that I be - long,
Am |Dm Em | Am |Dm   Em |
  Too many protest singers,   not enough protest songs.
     Am |Dm Em | Am |Dm Em
And now you've come along,   yes you've come along,
     Am |Dm   Am |
And I've never met a girl like you be - fore.

Guitar outro   As Intro chords ad lib. to end

© COPYRIGHT 1994 ISLAND MUSIC LIMITED.
UNIVERSAL/ISLAND MUSIC LIMITED.
ALL RIGHTS RESERVED. INTERNATIONAL COPYRIGHT SECURED.

Introduction

Edwyn Collins' 1994 hit single. One of those songs that sounds fresh no matter how many times you've heard it before.

Minor Chords

This song is a great one for working in those new minor chords. They are no harder really than the major shapes, but most people have a bit of a tussle with Dm. There is no secret to nailing this one, but getting in lots of your One-Minute Changes (BC-124) will definitely help.

One thing that is really important when you are learning a new tune is making sure that you know what the next chord is and how to play it. If you are trying to play it in time but aren't sure how many strums there are before the change or exactly how to play the next chord, the chances of playing it smoothly are about zero!

The 'And' after '2'

This tune has a very cool tied-rhythm pattern. This concept will be introduced in Stage 6, so don't rush into it too early (if you stick to the course you will make faster and more solid progress). The pattern used here is the one shown in BC-165 and is one of the most common rhythm patterns on the guitar. Note however that when there are two chords in a bar then the change happens on the first up-strum! So you play down, down on the first chord and up, up down on the second chord. A little tricky perhaps, but if you've been doing your homework it shouldn't take you too long to click with it.

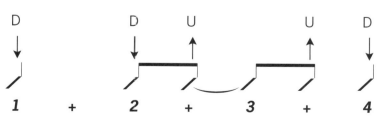

Louie Louie
Words & Music by Richard Berry

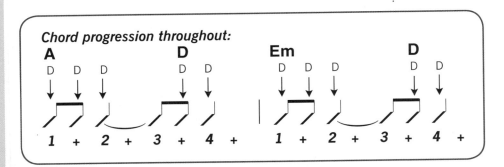

Chord progression throughout:

Chorus 1	Louie Louie, oh no, We gotta go, yeah, I said-a, Louie Louie, oh baby, We gotta go.
Verse 1	A fine little girl, she wait for me. Me catch a ship across the sea, Me sail a ship out all alone, Me never think how I'll make it home.
Chorus 2	As Chorus 1
Verse 2	Three nights and days I sailed the sea, I think of girl, oh, constantly. Oh, on that ship I dream she there, I smell the rose, ah, in her hair.
Chorus 3	As Chorus 1
Guitar solo	Chord progression x9
Verse 3	Me see Jamaican moon above, It won't be long me see me love. Me take her in my arms and then I tell her I'll never leave again.
Chorus 4	As Chorus 1
Outro	I said, we gotta go now, let's go.

© COPYRIGHT 1957 WINDSWEPT PACIFIC ENTERTAINMENT COMPANY D/B/A LONGITUDE MUSIC COMPANY, USA.
EMI MUSIC PUBLISHING (WP) LIMITED.
ALL RIGHTS RESERVED. INTERNATIONAL COPYRIGHT SECURED.

Introduction

'Louie Louie' is the stuff of rock 'n' roll legend—the lyrics here are the official version, but all sorts of obscenities have been interpreted to lurk within Kingsmen singer Jack Ely's slurred vocal performance.

Different Fingerings for Chords

When you play Em, try using different fingerings: either using fingers 1 and 2, 2 and 3 or 3 and 4 and see which one works best for you. With simple chords like this you do not have to stick to the same fingering all the time, as some songs and chord progressions will suit some fingerings better than others. As you progress you will have to learn to choose on the fly, so start now and feel out which one is best for you.

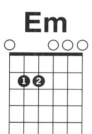
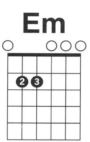
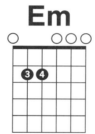

Strumming

The guitar part on the original recording was played with all down-strokes. I'm sure you'll pick it up if you listen to the record, but if you're struggling, count it out, as shown above the song. To start with you might like to try playing four-to-a-bar strums to get used to the chord changes, as follows:

A		D		Em		D	
D	D	D	D	D	D	D	D
↓	↓	↓	↓	↓	↓	↓	↓
1	+	2	+	3	+	4	+	1	+	2	+	3	+	4	+

I'd Rather Go Blind
Words & Music by Ellington Jordan, Billy Foster & Donto Foster

Capo Fret 7

Intro | D | Em | Em | D |

Verse 1
D   Em
Something told me it was o - ver, (yeah),
Em   D
When I saw you and her   talking.
D   Em
Something deep down in my soul said "cry girl,"
Em   D
When I saw you and that girl   walking out.

Chorus 1
D   Em
Ooh, I would rather, I would rather go blind, boy
Em   D
Than to see you walk away from me, child, no.
       D
Ooh, so you see I love you so much,
Em
But I don't want to watch you leave me, babe.
Em   D
Most of all, I just don't, I just don't want to be free, no.

Verse 2
Ooh, ooh, I was just, I was just,
I was just sitting here thinking
Of your kiss and your warm embrace, yeah.
When the reflection in the glass
That I held to my lips now, babe (yeah, yeah),
Revealed the tears
That was on my face, yeah, ooh.

Chorus 2
And baby, baby I'd rather,
I'd rather be blind, boy,
Than to see you walk away,
See you walk away from me, yeah, ooh.
Baby, baby, baby, I'd rather be blind now.

© COPYRIGHT 1967 ARC MUSIC CORPORATION, USA.
JEWEL MUSIC PUBLISHING COMPANY LIMITED.
ALL RIGHTS RESERVED. INTERNATIONAL COPYRIGHT SECURED.

⟳ Introduction
Etta James recorded this great soul song in 1968.

⟳ No Capo

Although we've stated here that you should play this song with the capo at the 7th fret—you only need to do that if you are going to play the Etta James version of the song. There are many different artists that have covered this song, so you might have to adjust the capo position if you want to play along with other versions. The best suggestion is to experiment with the first bit of the song. Start with the capo on the 1st fret, play along a bit and see if it sounds right; if it doesn't, start again with the capo or the 2nd fret and so on. Eventually you'll get the right fret (the most attempts it can take is twelve, including trying it without the capo!).

⟳ Loud and Soft

This song really works with just four down-strums per bar, but be aware of how loudly you are playing so that you can keep it quiet in the verse and louder in the chorus to keep it interesting for those listening.

D	D	D	D
↓	↓	↓	↓
/	/	/	/
1 +	2 +	3 +	4 +

Natural Mystic
Words & Music by Bob Marley

Intro

‖: Am | Am :‖ *Repeat ad lib.*

Chorus 1

       Dm   Em   Am   Am
There's a natural mystic blowing through the air;
       Dm   Em   Am   Am
If you listen carefu - lly now you will hear.
       Dm   Am   Dm   Am
This could be the first trumpet, might as well be the last:
      Dm   Am
Many more will have to suffer,
   | Dm   Em | Am   Dm | Am   Am |
Many more will have to die, don't ask me why.

Verse 1

Dm   Em   Am
Things are not the way they used to be,
| Am   Dm | Am   Am |
  I won't tell no lie.
      Dm   Em   Am   Am
One and all have to face reali - ty now.
       Dm   Am   Dm   Am
'Though I've tried to find the answer to all the questions they ask,
    Dm   Am | Dm Em | Am
'Though I know it's im - possible to go livin' through the past,
    Dm | Am   Am
Don't tell no lie.

Chorus 2

      Dm   Em   Am
There's a natural mystic blowing through the air,
| Am   Dm | Am   Am
   Can't keep them down.
      Dm   Em   Am   Am
If you listen care - fully now you will hear.
Am   Am   Am   Am
  There's a natural mystic,   blowing through the air.

Link

| Am | Am | Am | Am |

Verse 2

This could be the first trumpet, might as well be the last:
Many more will have to suffer,
Many more will have to die, don't ask me why.

Outro

There's a natural mystic blowing through the air, I won't tell no lie.
If you listen carefully now you will hear:
There's a natural mystic blowing through the air.
Such a natural mystic blowing through the air;
There's a natural mystic blowing through the air;
Such a natural mystic blowing through the air.

© COPYRIGHT 1977 BOB MARLEY MUSIC LIMITED.
BLUE MOUNTAIN MUSIC LIMITED.
ALL RIGHTS RESERVED. INTERNATIONAL COPYRIGHT SECURED.

Introduction

This minor-key Bob Marley song originally featured on his classic album *Exodus* (also see 'Three Little Birds' on page 8… you really ought to own this record!).

Dynamics

This song is a great one to get into exploring dynamics, by which I mean the 'louds' and 'softs' of the song. You can keep the strumming really simple—just four strums to a bar—but try and experiment with how loud you are playing. I think it sounds awesome playing really soft—it makes it kind of spooky—but then when you're feeling it you can turn the volume up (by strumming harder; don't touch you guitar volume if you're playing electric). It's a great skill to develop and dynamics can make simple things sound really cool, so be aware of them!

Strumming

To get a cool reggae groove going on here it's going to sound best if you do up-strums on the off-beats—beats 2 and 4. While tapping your foot on beats 1 and 3, it'll be foot tap, up-strum, foot tap, up-strum…

```
            U                    U
            ↑                    ↑
           /                    /
1    +    2    +    3    +    4    +
```

St. James Infirmary Blues
Traditional

Verse 1

|Am   E |Am |
I went down to St. James In - firmary.
|Am   Dm |E |
I saw my baby there.
|Am   E |Am |
Lying on a long white table,
 |Dm   E |Am |
So sweet, so cold, so fair.
|Am   E |Am |
I went up to see the doctor.
| Am   Dm |E |
"She's very low" he said.
 |Am   E |Am |
I went back to see my baby
          |Dm   E |Am |
And great God, she was lying there dead.

Verse 2

I went down to old Joe's barroom,
On the corner by the square
They were serving the drinks as usual,
And the usual crowd was there.
On my left stood old Joe McKennedy,
And his eyes were bloodshot red;
He turned to the crowd around him,
And these are the words he said:

Verse 3

"Let her go, let her go, God bless her;
Wherever she may be.
She may search the wide world over
And never find a better man than me."
Oh, when I die, please bury me
In my ten dollar Stetson hat;
Put a twenty-dollar gold piece on my watch chain
So my friends'll know I died standin' pat.

Verse 4

Get six gamblers to carry my coffin,
Six chorus girls to sing me a song.
Put a twenty-piece jazz band on my tail gate
To raise Hell as we go along.
Now that's the end of my story
So let's have another round of booze,
And if anyone should ask you just tell them
I've got the St. James Infirmary blues.

© COPYRIGHT 2011 DORSEY BROTHERS MUSIC LIMITED.
ALL RIGHTS RESERVED. INTERNATIONAL COPYRIGHT SECURED.

Introduction

This is a great minor-key blues standard, best imagined as a New Orleans-style funeral march. Recorded countless times by the classic jazz musicians such as Louis Armstrong, more contemporary renditions can be heard on the first White Stripes album and Hugh Laurie's album *Let Them Talk*. If you listen to some different versions you'll hear lots of different chord sequences for this song, but the melody and lyrics are recognizably the same.

 ## Jack White Version

The White Stripes version of this song just uses an Em chord (capo 1st fret) and a little single note run. Learning to hear things and work stuff out on your own is a great thing to do, so it's recommended that you have a go at working out that little line if you are a fan of the White Stripes! Just try it; working out stuff is a lot easier than most people think, and it's how many famous musicians learned to play.

 ## Stamp your Feet!

Strumming down on the beat for this song sounds great. This one needs to have a real thud to it, so stamping your foot on the beat will add to the groove and give it a really strong pulse. So rather than the usual silent soft-foot-tap, really give it a solid 'stomp' to give this one some energy!

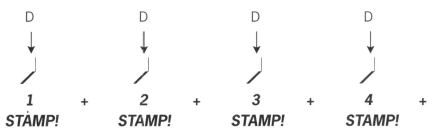

All Your Love (I Miss Loving)
Words & Music by Otis Rush

Intro

Am	Am	Am	Am
Dm	Dm	Am	Am
Em	Dm	Am	N.C.

Verse 1

(N.C.)   Am Am   Am Am
All the love in this loving,   all the kiss in this kissing.
               Dm Dm   Am Am
All the love in this loving,   all the kiss in this kissing.
           Em Dm   Am   N.C.
Before I met you baby, never knew what I were missing.

Verse 2

All your love, pretty baby, that I got in store for you.
All your love, pretty baby, that I got in store for you.
I love you pretty baby, well I say you love me too.

Solo

As Intro chords

Verse 3

All your loving, pretty baby, all your loving, pretty baby.
All your loving, pretty baby, all your loving, pretty baby.
Since I first met you baby, I never knew what I were missing.

Verse 4

Hey, hey baby, hey, hey baby.
Yeah, yeah, yeah, yeah, yeah, baby, oh, oh, baby.
Since I first met you baby, never knew what I were missing.

Outro

As Intro chords

© COPYRIGHT 1965 CONRAD MUSIC, A DIVISION OF ARC MUSIC CORPORATION, USA.
TRISTAN MUSIC LIMITED.
ALL RIGHTS RESERVED. INTERNATIONAL COPYRIGHT SECURED.

Introduction

This 60s blues-revival song featured on *John Mayall's Bluesbreakers With Eric Clapton* album (1966), nicknamed the 'Beano' album, as a young Slowhand is reading a copy (upside down!) of the UK comic on the cover shot.

Original Riffs

The original recording of this song has some really cool riffs in it. After you have finished the 12-Bar Blues Variation in Stage 9, you might like to go listen and see if you can work out how to play those riffs. You will know what the notes are, so you will just have to work out the order to play them in. You will be amazed at how much you have grown as a guitar player by the end of Stage 9 as well, so it's always fun to look back to songs you learned before and see how far you have come!

 ## Shufflin'

Yet another song you can have fun with later on! You can play this tune with many different patterns, but probably the coolest is to use the shuffle strumming taught in BC-156: divide each beat into 3 and play the first and last of each group of triplets, as shown here.

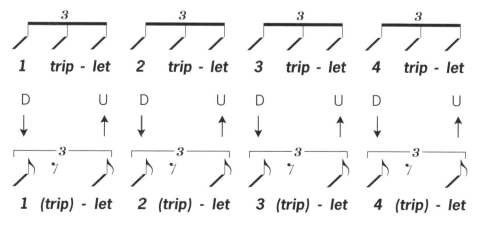

Twist And Shout

Words & Music by Bert Russell & Phil Medley

Capo Fret 5

Intro	| A D E | A D E |

Chorus 1	**A** **D** **E**
	Well, shake it up, baby now, (shake it up, baby,)
	      A **D** **E**
	Twist and shout, (twist and shout.)
	                    A **D** **E**
	C'mon, c'mon, c'mon, c'mon baby now, (come on baby,)
	            A **D** **E**
	Come on and work it on out, (work it on out.)

Verse 1	Well, work it on out, (work it on out,) You know you look so good, (look so good.) You know you got me goin' now, (got me goin',) Just like I knew you would, (like I knew you would.)
Chorus 2	As Chorus 1
Verse 2	You know you twist it, little girl, (twist little girl,) You know you twist so fine, (twist so fine.) Come on and twist a little closer now, (twist a little closer,) And let me know that you're mine, (let me know you're mine, ooh.)
Middle	| A D | E D | A D | E D | | A D | E D | A D | E | **E E E E E E** Ah, ah, ah, ah._____
Chorus 3	As Chorus 1
Verse 3	As Verse 2
Outro	Well, shake it, shake it, shake it baby now, (shake it up baby,) Well, shake it, shake it, shake it baby now, (shake it up baby,) Well, shake it, shake it, shake it baby now, (shake it up baby,) Ah, ah, ah, ah.

© COPYRIGHT 1960 SONY/ATV MUSIC PUBLISHING.
ALL RIGHTS RESERVED. INTERNATIONAL COPYRIGHT SECURED.

Introduction

Usually associated with The Beatles' raucous version, this rock 'n' roll standard was first a hit for The Isley Brothers in 1962.

Singing and Playing

Most people who learn guitar want to sing and play at the same time. The trick is to understand that you can't think about two things at once. So, one of the things you're doing has to be on auto-pilot; for 99% of people, the guitar part will be the thing that has to work on its own. A song like this with three chords that repeat throughout is a good one to practise this with. You won't be able to do it if you are still struggling with the changes, but when you can play the guitar parts without thinking about them, have a crack at singing too!

Syncopated Strumming

The pattern that works best for this song is quite *syncopated*. What does that mean? Well, lets just say it's a bit tricky for Stage 2, but should be fine by the time you have worked with the concepts of ties in Stage 7. Just be content with your simple strumming for now—it will still sound cool—and come back to this more authentic two-bar syncopated pattern (shown below) when you are more confident with ties and missing beats.

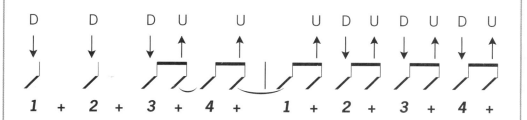

Peggy Sue
Words & Music by Buddy Holly, Norman Petty & Jerry Allison

Intro

‖: A D | A E :‖

Verse 1

A   D |A   D |A
If you knew Peggy Sue, then you'd know why I feel blue
         D D |A D A
Without Peggy, my Peggy Sue.____
             E   D |A D |A E |
Oh well, I love you gal, yes, I love you, Peggy Sue.____

Verse 2

Peggy Sue, Peggy Sue, oh how my heart yearns for you,
Oh Peggy, my Peggy Sue.
Oh well, I love you gal, yes I love you, Peggy Sue.

Chorus 1

A   A
Peggy Sue, Peggy Sue,
F   A
Pretty, pretty, pretty, pretty Peggy Sue
    D |A D |A
Oh Peggy, my Peggy Sue,____
          E
Oh well, I love you gal,
    D |A D |A E |
Yes I need you, Peggy Sue.____

Verse 3

I love you, Peggy Sue, With a love so rare and true,
Oh Peggy, my Peggy Sue,
Well, I love you gal, I want you, Peggy Sue.

Instrumental

A	D	A D A	D A D A
D	D	A D	A
E	D	A D	A E

Chorus 2

As Chorus 1

Verse 4

As Verse 3

Outro

          E
Oh well, I love you gal,
    D |A D |A |
And I want you Peggy Sue.____

© COPYRIGHT 1957 MPL COMMUNICATIONS INCORPORATED, USA.
PEERMUSIC (UK) LIMITED.
ALL RIGHTS RESERVED. INTERNATIONAL COPYRIGHT SECURED.

Introduction

One of Buddy Holly's biggest-ever hits, this was released as a single in 1957.

The 'Cheating' F Chord

This song has an F chord in the chorus, which is quite a tricky chord to play, but this song is so much fun to practise your A, D and E chords on that I didn't want to move it to later in the course. So we can do a very naughty cheat. Just move the E chord up one fret and try to only play the strings that your fingers are on, so none of the open strings ring out. It's not a good way to play F in the long run and eventually you should learn how to play F properly. This is just a little cheat to get you going!

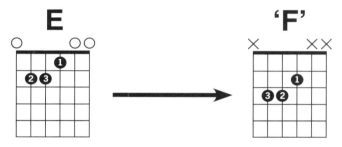

Strumming

This song is played with all down-strums, which can be quite a challenge to play fast. So slow down! If you are new to playing don't be in a hurry to play things fast, just take your time, do it right and the speed will develop. A good way to start is by strumming at half speed.

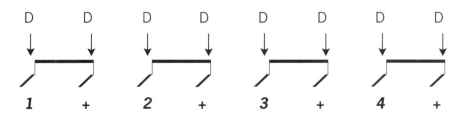

Lay Down Sally

Words & Music by Eric Clapton, George Terry & Marcy Levy

Intro
‖: A | A7 | A | A7 :‖ Play x4

Verse 1
A   A
There is nothing that is wrong
A   A   D   D
With wanting you to stay here with me.
A   A
I know you've got some - where to go
A   A   D   D
But won't you make your - self at home and stay with me
      E   E
And don't you ever leave.

Chorus 1
A A D   D
Lay down Sally, and rest here in my arms.
E   E   A A
Don't you think you want someone to talk to?
A A D   D
Lay down Sally, no need to leave so soon,
E   E   A A
I've been trying all night long just to talk to you.

Link
‖: A | A7 | A | A7 :‖

Verse 2
Sun ain't nearly on the rise,
We still got the moon and stars above.
Underneath the velvet skies
Love is all that matters, won't you stay with me?
And don't you ever leave.

Chorus 2
As Chorus 1

Solo
‖: A | A | A | A :‖ Play x8

Verse 3
I love to see the morning light
Colouring your face so dreamily.
So don't you go and say goodbye,
You can lay your worries down and stay with me,
And don't you ever leave.

Chorus 3
As Chorus 1

© COPYRIGHT 1977 & 1999 WARNER/CHAPPELL MUSIC LIMITED/ERIC CLAPTON.
ALL RIGHTS RESERVED. INTERNATIONAL COPYRIGHT SECURED.

Introduction

A country-flavoured excursion for Eric Clapton from his *Slowhand* LP (1977).

A to A7

The intro and link sections in this song use an A chord followed by an A7 chord. If you are using my suggested fingering (1.) for an A chord, changing to A7 is as simple as lifting off your 1st finger! If you use the other common fingering for the A (2.) then you would lift up your 2nd finger to get the A7. See what works for you. It's OK to be different and we all get some things easier than others, so part of the journey is working out what works for you.

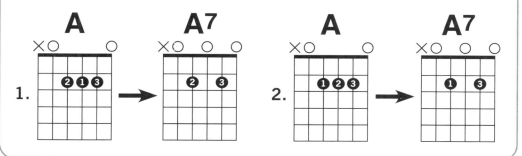

Strumming

You can play this with regular strumming but it sounds awesome with the 12-Bar Shuffle playing shown in BC-183, and even cooler using the variations in BC-194. However, to learn the tune and get going, just use a regular strum:

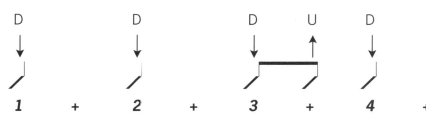

Wild Thing
Words & Music by Chip Taylor

Intro
| A   D | E |

Chorus 1
A   D E
Wild thing,
D   A   D E
You make my heart sing,
D   A   D   E
You make everything groovy,
D A   D
    Wild thing.

Link 1
| E   G⁶ A G⁶ |

Verse 1
A N.C.   G⁶ A G⁶
Wild thing I think I love you
A N.C.   G⁶ A G⁶
But I want to know for sure.
A N.C.   G⁶ A G⁶
So come on and hold me tight.
A N.C.
I love you.

Link 2
| A   D | E   D | A   D | E   D |

Chorus 2
As Chorus 1

Recorder Solo
| A   D | E   D | A   D | E   D |
| A   D | E   D | A   D | E   G⁶ A G⁶ |

Verse 2
Wild thing I think you move me
But I wanna know for sure.
So come on and hold me tight.
You move me.

Link 3
| A   D | E   D | A   D | E | E | E | E |

Chorus 3
As Chorus 1

Chorus 4
D   A   D
Come on, come on, wild thing.
E D   A   D | E | E | E |
   Shake it, shake it, wild thing.   Ahh.

© COPYRIGHT 1966 EMI BLACKWOOD MUSIC INCORPORATED, USA.
EMI SONGS LTD.
ALL RIGHTS RESERVED. INTERNATIONAL COPYRIGHT SECURED.

Introduction

The Troggs' 'Wild Thing' was given a brutal makeover by Jimi Hendrix on his *Live At Monteray* album. This sounds great on cranked-up electric (setting your guitar on fire like Jimi strictly optional…).

The easy way to play G6!

This song uses a G6 chord, and there is a nice little way to play it. Playing the open strings gives a kind of G6 chord, so to play the verse riff, finger an A chord, then lift your fingers off to play the open strings—i.e., G6—then put them back down, play the A, lift them off for the G6 and then back down again, taking care not to hit the thickest strings.

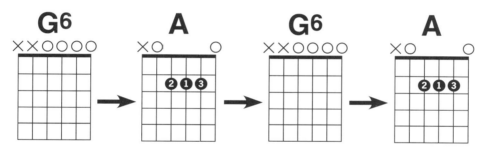

Wild Rhythm

Everyone knows how the rhythm for this song goes, and it's actually easier to just mimic the record rather than counting the rhythm. So, just play the rhythm with all down-strums and worry about what you are really doing later on. If you want to count it, try it like this, leaving the bracketed 3 as a whisper: '1, 2, (3), and 4.' Once you can say it, try and play it, sticking with all down-strums.

STAGE 3 BC-131—BC-139

 Introduction

We introduce a couple of new chords in this stage which require a bit of a stretch and many people find them tricky to change between at first. This is really normal so don't worry about it. Getting these chords right is just down to practice; I suggest doing lots of One-Minute Changes (BC-134) to help you improve.

We also have our first proper strumming pattern (BC-136) to try and mix in. You will need to practise it on a single chord so much that it becomes automatic for you when you want to use in a song:

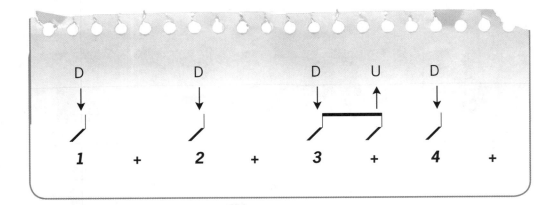

This last point is VERY important. The students who progress the fastest are those that separate their work on chord changes from practising rhythm patterns like this one. So, keep using the 'boring' four-strums-per bar for songs to really nail the chord changes, while working separately on rhythm patterns on a single chord until they are natural and instinctive. Then, you can play the changes with the new patterns, as you will be comfortable with both.

In fact, you should only start using the rhythm patterns when you can play through a song with four strums per bar with the metronome, without stopping for any of the chord changes. It requires patience, but really works. I hope you have more patience than I did when I was learning!

Quite a few songs in this stage are shown with a strum pattern that uses a tie. We're going to look at this pattern a little later in Stage 6 (many of my students call it "old faithful" because it nearly always sounds good and is used all the time), so you should revisit these songs in the future and apply that pattern. You will notice that it sounds a lot more natural than the four-to-the-bar strumming—but you are not going to rush into it yet, are you?

Stage 3 Chords

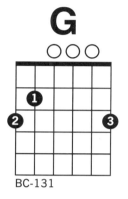
G
BC-131

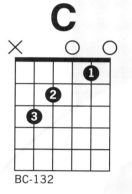
C
BC-132

Stage 3: Your notes

Hey Joe
Words & Music by Billy Roberts

Chord progression throughout:
| C G | D A | E | E |

Verse 1
Hey Joe, where you goin' with that gun of yours?
Hey Joe, I said where you goin' with that gun in your hand?
I'm goin' down to shoot my lady,
You know I caught her messin' 'round with another man.
Yeah, I'm goin' down to shoot my ol' lady,
You know I caught her messin' 'round with another man
Huh! And that ain't too cool.

Verse 2
A-hey Joe, I heard you shot your woman down, you shot her down now.
A-hey Joe, I heard you shot your old lady down,
You shot her down in the ground, yeah!
Yes, I did, I shot her,
You know I caught her messin' 'round, messin' 'round town,
Uh, yes I did, I shot her.
You know I caught my old lady messin' 'round town,
Then I gave her the gun,
I shot her.

Solo
As Verse Chords

Verse 3
Hey Joe, where you gonna run to now, where you gonna run to?
"Hey Joe", I said, "Where you gonna run to now, where you gonna go?"
I'm goin' way down South, way down to Mexico way.
I'm goin' way down South, way down where I can be free,
Ain't no one gonna find me.

Outro
Ain't no hang-man gonna,
He ain't gonna put a rope around me,
You better believe it right now,
I gotta go now,
Hey Joe, you better run on down,
Goodbye everybody. Ow!

© COPYRIGHT 1962 THIRD STORY MUSIC COMPANY INCORPORATED, USA.
CARLIN MUSIC CORPORATION.
ALL RIGHTS RESERVED. INTERNATIONAL COPYRIGHT SECURED.

Introduction

Synonymous with Jimi Hendrix, (but actually credited to Billy Roberts) whose studio version on *Are You Experienced* is essential listening. There are also several famous live versions, not least the festival-closing performance from Woodstock.

All the Majors

This is a great song for working on all your major chord grips. You have all five grips, one after the other in this song, so as well as being a cool tune, it's also a great chord workout.

Strumming

Jimi Hendrix's style on this kind of song was very much a mixture of lead and rhythm playing, so there is not really a set strumming pattern for this song—but this one will work very well:

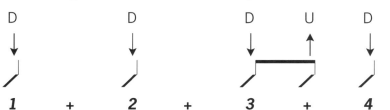

The ending riff of this song is awesome, so we've included it in tab here too. If you have not learned to read tab yet, just come back to it later. It also makes a cool finger-exercise and is good for working on your single-note-picking. Use whatever fingers you like, and play all down-picks for now.

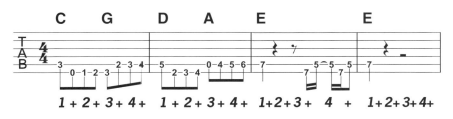

Mad World

Words & Music by Roland Orzabal

Capo Fret 1

Intro

| Em | A | Em | A |

Verse 1

Em   G
All around me are familiar faces,
D   A
Worn out places, worn out faces.
Em   G
Bright and early for their daily races,
D   A
Going nowhere, going nowhere.
Em   G
And their tears are filling up their glasses,
D   A
No expression, no expression.
Em   G
Hide my head I want to drown my sorrow,
D   A
No tomorrow, no tomorrow.

Pre-chorus 1

Em   A   Em
And I find it kind of funny, I find it kind of sad.
                      A   Em
The dreams in which I'm dying, are the best I've ever had.
                A   Em
I find it hard to tell you, I find it hard to take.
                    A
When people run in circles, It's a very, very...

Chorus 1

Em   A   Em   A
   Mad world,   mad world.

Verse 2

Children waiting for the day they feel good,
Happy Birthday, Happy Birthday!
Made to feel the way that every child should,
Sit and listen, sit and listen.
Went to school and I was very nervous,
No one knew me, no one knew me.
"Hello teacher, tell me what's my lesson?"
Look right through me, look right through me.

Pre-chorus 2

As Pre-chorus 1

Chorus 2

Mad World, mad world.
Enlarging your world, mad world.

© COPYRIGHT 1982 ROLAND ORZABAL LIMITED.
CHRYSALIS MUSIC LIMITED.
ALL RIGHTS RESERVED. INTERNATIONAL COPYRIGHT SECURED.

Introduction

Written by Tears For Fears in 1982 and re-interpreted in a minimalist style by Gary Jules and Michael Andrews for the cult movie *Donnie Darko*, this became a surprise UK Christmas No. 1 in 2003.

Playing With Sensitivity

This lovely ballad is arranged to play along with the Gary Jules recording, with a capo on the 1st fret. The trick with this type of song is to play it sensitively, so keep the strumming nice and soft. Once you have covered some basic patterns in Stage 9, you can play this song fingerstyle, picking out individual notes, just like the piano does on the recording. To play along with the Tears For Fears version you'll need a capo on the 2nd fret, although given the electronic nature of that version, I find that the guitar doesn't blend in nearly as well.

Strumming

This song can work with many different strumming patterns, but start by keeping it very simple, just playing 4 strums to the bar. Once you've done that you can add in the 'ands' after beats 2 and 3 so you have the pattern shown below. Later in the course you might like to try using 'Old Faithful'—which you will learn soon—and which will be very easy if you have practised the pattern below!

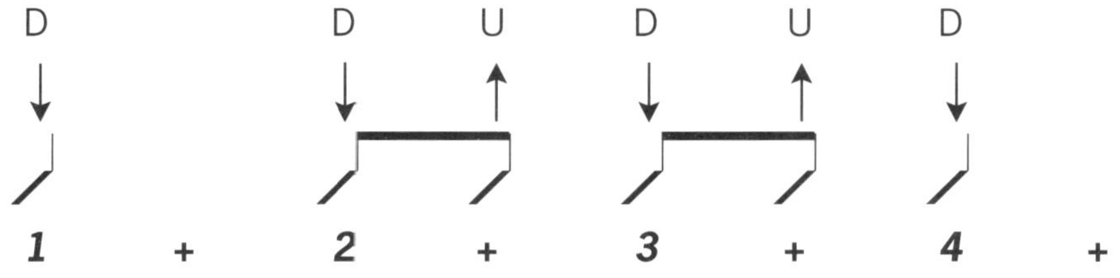

```
D        D   U    D   U    D
↓        ↓   ↑    ↓   ↑    ↓
1   +    2   +    3   +    4   +
```

Hey Ya!
Words & Music by André Benjamin

Verse 1

1, 2, 3, Uh!
```
G              C
My baby don't mess around
             C                         |D    |E    E
Because she loves me so and this I know fo' sho' (Uh!)
G              C
   But does she really wanna
            C                           |D    |E    E
Not to ex - pect to see me walk out the do'?
G              C
   Don't try to fight the feeling
           C                          |D    |E    E
'Cause the thought alone is killing me right now. (Uh!)
G                    C                              C
   Thank God for Mom and Dad for sticking two together
       |D    |E    E
'Cause we don't know how. C'mon!
```

Chorus 1
```
G   C     C |D |E   E
Hey Ya!    Hey Ya! (Play x4)
```

Verse 2

You think you've got it oh, you think you've got it,
But got it just don't get it
'Til there's nothing at all. (Ah!)
We get together oh, we get together
But separate's always better
When there's feelings involved. (Oh!)
If what they say is "nothing is forever"
Then what makes, then what makes, then what makes,
Then what makes, then what makes, (What makes? What makes?)
Love the exception?
So why oh, why oh
Why oh, why oh, why oh are we so in denial
When we know we're not happy here?

Chorus 2

Hey Ya! Hey Ya! (*Play x4*)

© COPYRIGHT 2003 GNAT BOOTY MUSIC, USA.
CHRYSALIS MUSIC LIMITED.
ALL RIGHTS RESERVED. INTERNATIONAL COPYRIGHT SECURED.

Introduction

An effortless pop classic from Andre 3000's half of Outkast's *Speakerboxx/The Love Below* double album.

Unusual Timing

This song has a 2/4 bar in it, which means that bar has only two beats in it instead of the usual four. It's cool to play but it may take you a little time to get used to it, because it might feel a little strange. Try putting on the original recording and count along with it, just so you get a feel for how the chords change.

Strumming

This one uses one of the most common strumming patterns of all time, except for the 2/4 bars, which take just two down-strums.

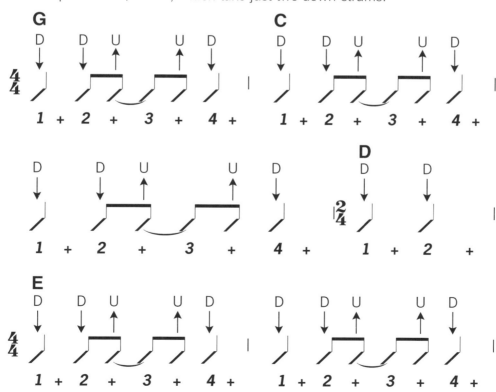

Brown Eyed Girl
Words & Music by Van Morrison

Intro $\|$: G | C | G | D :$\|$

Verse 1
G   C   G   D
Hey, where did we go   Days when the rains came?
G   C   G   D
Down in the hollow,   Playing a new game.
G   C   G   D
Laughing and a runnin', hey hey,   Skipping and a - jumpin'
G   C   G   D
In the misty morning fog with   Our, our hearts a - thumpin' and.
C   D   G   Em
You, my brown eyed girl.
C   D   G D
And you, my   brown eyed girl.

Verse 2
And what ever happened to Tuesday and so slow?
Going down to the old mine with a transistor radio.
Standing in the sunlight laughing, hiding behind a rainbow's wall.
Slipping and a - sliding all along the waterfall with
You, my brown eyed girl.
You, my brown eyed girl.

Chorus 1
D   D   D
Do you re - member when   we used to sing
G   C   G   D
Sha la la la la la la, la la la la de da. (x2)

Verse 3
So hard to find my way, now that I'm all on my own
I saw you just the other day, my how you have grown
Cast my memory back there, Lord,
Sometimes I'm overcome thinkin' about it
Makin' love in the green grass, behind the stadium with
You, my brown eyed girl.
You, my brown eyed girl.

Chorus 2   As Chorus 1 to fade

© COPYRIGHT 1967 WEB IV MUSIC INCORPORATED, USA.
UNIVERSAL MUSIC PUBLISHING LIMITED.
ALL RIGHTS RESERVED. INTERNATIONAL COPYRIGHT SECURED.

Introduction

One of Van Morrison's best-known songs, and a sure-fire sing-along!

Strumming

This very common pattern works perfectly in this song pretty much all the way through. For the D Chord in the "Do you remember when…" part you might want to switch to all down-strums and get louder and louder to build into the chorus. A pro touch!

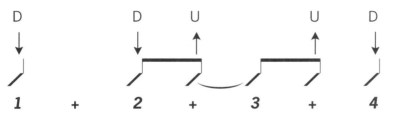

Intro Riff

This is an all-time classic guitar riff. Start using your 1st and 2nd fingers and keep your 1st finger on the thinnest string for the whole riff (until bar 4). You should use your 1st and 3rd fingers when there is a fret gap between the notes. In bar 4, use your 1st and 4th fingers for the first two notes and then fingers 1, 2 and then 4 for the rest!

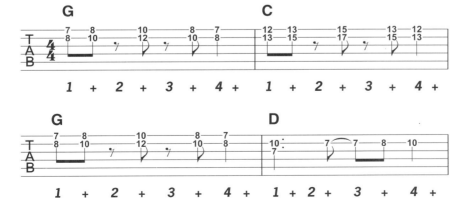

Yellow Submarine
Words & Music by John Lennon & Paul McCartney

Verse 1

| **D**   **C** |**G**   **Em** |
In the town where I was born, lived a
Am   **C** |**D**   **G** |
Man who sailed to sea, and he
D   **C** |**G**   **Em** |
Told us of his life, in the
Am   **C** |**D** |
Land of subma - rines. (So we)

Verse 2

So we sailed up to the sun, till we
Found the sea of green, and we
Lived beneath the waves, in our
Yellow submarine.

Chorus 1

G   **D**
We all live in a yellow submarine,
D   **G**
Yellow submarine, yellow submarine.
G   **D**
We all live in a yellow submarine,
D   **G**
Yellow submarine, yellow submarine.

Verse 3

And our friends are all aboard, many
More of them live next door, and the
Band begins to play.

Link

| **G**   **G** | **D**   **G** |

Chorus 2

As Chorus 1

Instrumental

| **D**   **C** **G**   **Em**| **Am**   **C** | **D**   **G** |
| **D**   **C** **G**   **Em**| **Am**   **C** | **D**   **G** |

Verse 4

As we live a life of ease, every
One of us has all we need, sky of
Blue and sea of green, in our
Yellow submarine.

Chorus 3

As Chorus 1 *(Repeat to fade)*

© COPYRIGHT 1966 SONY/ATV MUSIC PUBLISHING.
ALL RIGHTS RESERVED. INTERNATIONAL COPYRIGHT SECURED.

Introduction

The Beatles' psychedelic vehicle—along with 'With A Little Help From My Friends', this was one of the biggest Beatles hits to feature a Ringo Starr lead vocal. The tuning on the original record is someway off normal pitch, so it's best not to try and play along with this one!

Single Strum

In this tune, the verses sound really cool if you strum each chord just once. Strum on beats 1 and 4. In the first verse, the first chord (D) will fall on beat 1. The next chord, C, (above 'I') will fall on beat 4, the G ('born') on beat 1, and so on. For the chorus, try the second pattern shown below.

Chorus strumming

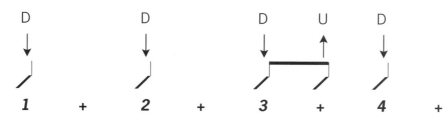

Somebody To Love

Words & Music by Darby Slick

Capo Fret 2

Verse 1
```
         Em              |A  D   |Em    Em
When the truth is found     to be      lies
         Em              |A  D   |Em    Em
And all the joy   with-in you         dies.
```

Chorus 1
```
N.C.    |G        D    |Em    A     |
Don't you want some-body to love,  don't you
G        D    |Em    A     |
Need some-body to love, wouldn't you
G        D    |Em    A     |
Love some-body to love, you'd better
D        A    |(Em)
find some-body to love.
```

Link 1
```
| Em   | A   | Em   | D   | Em   | Em   ||
```

Verse 2
When the garden flowers, they are dead, yes,
And your mind, your mind, is so full of red.

Chorus 2   As Chorus 1

Verse 3
```
N.C.                                        |D   A    |
Your eyes, I say your eyes may look like his,     yeah, but
Em         |A     D         |Em         Em
In your head, ba-by, I'm afr-aid you don't know where it is.
```

Chorus 3   As Chorus 1

Link 2
```
| Em   | D   | A   | G   | Em   | Em   ||
```

Verse 4
Tears are running all round and round your breast,
And your friends, baby, they treat you like a guest.

Chorus 4
```
                             D     |G        D    |A         |G        D    |A
Don't you want some-body to love, don't you need some-body to love,
                             |G        D    |A
Wouldn't you love some-body to love,
                             |D        A    |Em   A   A   A
You'd better find some-body to love. _____
```

Coda
```
            Solo
| Em   | Em   || Em   | A   | Em   | A   |
| Em   | A  D | Em   | Em   | G  D | A   |
| G  D | A    | G  D | A    | G  A ||
```

62

Introduction

One of the defining psychedelic rock songs, this was the first and biggest hit for Jefferson Airplane, a band so trippy they called their first album *Surrealistic Pillow*. It's also a cracking rock song with a chorus you can really belt out!

Chopping Beats

A classic song and lots of fun to play. Watch out for the N.C. (No Chord) break in Verse 3, because the bar before the guitar comes in is only two beats long. So, you will have to count one bar of four, and then one bar of six beats. It was quite common in this era to chop off a few beats in order to fit the vocal melody, and it can be strange to get used to, so don't worry if you find it a little tricky. It's only important to get this right if you're playing along with the original recording—if you're playing without the recording, you may find it easier to count three bars of four beats, which will sound more 'regular'.

Strumming

Start this tune by keeping the strumming very simple and playing down-strums on the beat. Be sure to start like this before you try to copy the strumming on the recording, which has some very interesting rhythms going on. Below I have put a pattern that works most of the way through the song, but if you are a more advanced player you might like to keep an ear out for the 'pushes', where chords change just before the next bar.

The pattern below is two bars long, and you should note that where there are two chords per bar, the change in the second bar will happen on the 'and' between beats 2 and 3, which is an up-strum. It gives it a really cool groove but will almost certainly be tricky for beginner players! Make sure you have the easy strumming really solid before you try any of the more advanced patterns.

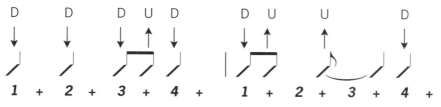

How To Save A Life
Words & Music by Joseph King & Isaac Slade

Capo Fret **3**

Intro | G | D | G | D |

Verse 1
     G   D
Step one, you say we need to talk,
  G   D   G
He walks, you say "Sit down, it's just a talk."
            D
He smiles po - litely back at you,
  G   D   G
   You stare po - litely right on through
        D   G
Some sort of window to your right,
        D   G
As he goes left and you stay right.
           D   G
Between the lines of fear and blame,
        D
You begin to wonder why you came.

Chorus 1
  C   D   Em
Where did I go wrong, I lost a friend
        | G   D |
Somewhere a - long in the bitterness.
      C   D   Em
And I would have stayed up with you all night,
     | G   D | G |
Had I known how to save a life.

Link 1 | G | D | G | D |

Verse 2
Let him know that you know best,
'Cause after all you do know best.
Try to slip past his defence
Without granting innocence.
Lay down a list of what is wrong,
The things you've told him all along.
Pray to God he hears you
And pray to God he hears you.

Chorus 2 As Chorus 1

Link 2 | G | D | Em | D |

© COPYRIGHT 2005 EMI MUSIC PUBLISHING LIMITED.
ALL RIGHTS RESERVED. INTERNATIONAL COPYRIGHT SECURED.

Verse 3
As he begins to raise his voice,
You lower yours and grant him one last choice.
Drive until you lose the road
Or break with the ones you've followed.
He will do one of two things,
He will admit to everything
Or he'll say he's just not the same
And you'll begin to wonder why you came.

Chorus 3
(Repeat Chorus to end)

Introduction

This inspirational hit by The Fray was released in 2006. The original is heavily piano-based, but the chords sound great on guitar as well.

Strumming

This song has been pretty heavily simplified but sounds cool. The main things that have been changed are the bass notes of the chords. This is not a big deal and you can still play and sing along with the original and make it sound cool. Although there is guitar on the recording, the dominant sound you hear is piano, which is playing pretty complicated stuff. This means you have a lot of freedom when it comes to the strumming pattern you choose. I'm suggesting you just use 'Old Faithful'…

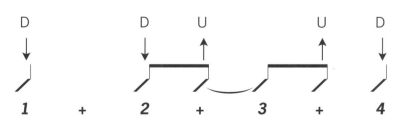

What's Up?
Words & Music by Linda Perry

Capo Fret 2

Chord progression throughout:
| G | Am | C | G |

Verse 1
25 years of my life and still
I'm trying to get up that great big hill of hope
For a destination.

And I realised quickly when I knew I should
That the world was made up of this
Brotherhood of man, for whatever that means.

Pre-chorus 1
And so I cry sometimes when I'm lying in bed
Just to get it all out, what's in my head
And I, I am feeling a little peculiar.

And so I wake in the morning and I step outside
And I take a deep breath and I get real high
And I scream from the top of my lungs, "What's goin' on?"

Chorus 1
And I say, "Hey, yeah, yeah, yeah, Hey, yeah, yeah."
I said "Hey, what's goin' on?"

Link 1
As Verse chords

Verse 2
And I try, oh my God do I try,
I try all the time in this institution.

And I pray, oh my God do I pray,
I pray every single day for a revolution.

Pre-chorus 2
As Pre-chorus 1

Chorus 2
As Chorus 1 *(Play x2)*

Link 2
As Verse chords

Outro
25 years and my life is still,
I'm trying to get up that great big hill of hope
For a destination.

© COPYRIGHT 1993 STUCK IN THE THROAT/FAMOUS MUSIC LLC, USA.
SONY/ATV HARMONY.
ALL RIGHTS RESERVED. INTERNATIONAL COPYRIGHT SECURED.

Introduction

4 Non Blondes singer Linda Perry is a successful songwriter for other artists, notably Christina Aguilera and Pink. This was her former band's biggest hit in 1993.

Capo

This song was originally played using the chords A, Bm and D, but we won't look at Bm yet because it's usually played as a barre chord (covered in the Intermediate Method). By using a capo on the 2nd fret we can get the same sounding chords playing G, Am and C. So you can see, using a capo can really simplify things!

Strumming

The strumming for this song is a two-bar pattern, and it's a really cool one. It takes practice to get these two-bar patterns internalized so that they come out without thinking about it. There is no trick to this though —it'll only come by doing it over and over again.

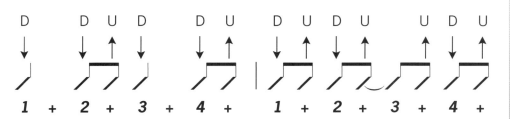

This Year's Love
Words & Music by David Gray

Capo Fret 1

Verse 1

```
C        D              C          D            C
This year's love had better last,   Heaven knows it's high time
      D            G    |G     Em  |
And I've been waiting on my own too long
C        D                    C            D
But when you hold me like you do, it feels so right
C      D            G           G
I start to forget, how my heart gets torn
          Em      Em         A           C    C
When that hurt gets thrown, feeling like you can't go on.
```

Verse 2

```
C        D                   C           D
Turning circles when time a - gain, it cuts like a knife oh, now
C      D        G    |G     Em  |
If you love me got to know for sure
C         D                    C                D
'Cos it takes something more this time, than sweet, sweet lies oh, now
C      D           G        G             Em        Em
Before I open up my arms and fall, losing all con - trol
        A            C              C
Every dream inside my soul and when you kiss me
          G        G          Em        Em
On that midnight street, sweep me off my feet
          A         C         C
Singing ain't this life so sweet.
```

Chorus

```
C        D              C         D
This year's love had better last

|C       |D       |G       |G      Em |
```

Outro

```
C        D              C   D  C           D
This year's love had better last,    'cause who's to worry
         G        G           Em       Em
If our hearts get torn when that hurt gets thrown
          A              C                    C
Don't you know this life goes on, and won't you kiss me
          G        G          Em        Em
On that midnight street, sweep me off my feet,
          A         C
Singing ain't this life so sweet
  C        D              C         D
|: This year's love had better last.    :|  Play x4
```

© COPYRIGHT 1998 CHRYSALIS MUSIC LIMITED.
ALL RIGHTS RESERVED. INTERNATIONAL COPYRIGHT SECURED.

Introduction
This David Gray song featured in the movie of the same name in 1999.

 ## Strumming

This song has a 6/8 time signature, meaning there are two beats in the bar and each beat is divided into 3. In unusual time signatures it can really help to count along. In this song you will count to 6 for each chord and should start with just a strum on the 1 and the 4. If you want to try the 6 strums per bar then make sure you accent the strums with the count of 1 anc 4, it will really help it roll. I strongly advise learning to count rhythms out loud, it really helps as you encounter harder rhythms!

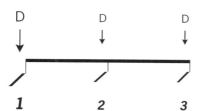 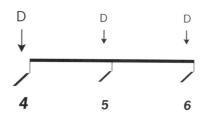

Working Class Hero

Words & Music by John Lennon

Verse 1

    Am   Am   G   Am Am Am Am
As soon as you're born they make you feel small,
    Am   Am   G   Am Am Am Am
By giving you no time in - stead of it all,
     Am   Am   G   Am Am Am Am
'Til the pain is so big you feel nothing at all.

Chorus 1

   Am   Am   G   Am Am Am Am
A working class hero is something to be,
   Am   G   D   Am Am Am Am
A working class hero is something to be.

Verse 2

They hurt you at home and they hit you at school,
They hate you if you're clever and they despise a fool,
'Til you're so ****ing crazy you can't follow their rules.

Chorus 2

As Chorus 1

Verse 3

When they've tortured and scared you for twenty odd years,
Then they expect you to pick a career,
When you can't really function you're so full of fear.

Chorus 3

As Chorus 1

Verse 4

Keep you doped with religion and sex and T.V.
And you think you're so clever and classless and free,
But you're still ****ing peasants as far as I can see.

Chorus 4

As Chorus 1

Verse 5

There's room at the top they are telling you still,
But first you must learn how to smile as you kill,
If you want to be like the folks on the hill.

Chorus 5

As Chorus 1

Chorus 6

If you want to be a hero well just follow me,
If you want to be a hero well just follow me.

© COPYRIGHT 1970 SONY/ATV MUSIC PUBLISHING.
ALL RIGHTS RESERVED. INTERNATIONAL COPYRIGHT SECURED.

Introduction

John Lennon's scornful broadside at class divisions still resonates today as strongly as it did on his 1970 *John Lennon/Yoko Ono Band* album. The more things change…

Playing in 3/4

The rhythms in this song are a little unusual—it's in 3/4, meaning there are 3 beats in a bar, and the strum pattern for each bar is shown below, with the count of 1 2+ 3+ (D DU DU).

The song is written out so that you will play one bar of 3/4 for each time a chord is written. I know it looks strange to see the Am written so many times, but I'm sure it will help you get it right. Make sure you listen to it and follow along with the chords with your finger on the page, that should really help make it all clear!

Strumming

This song is a great one to learn now; get the chords all sorted and then revisit it after you have looked at the bass note-pick-strum pattern in Stage 7 (specifically lesson BC-175). It's a little different because this song is in 3/4; the pattern would normally be played bass note, down-up, down-up. The bass note on the Am moves between the root note (fifth string, open) and the E note (fourth string, 2nd fret).

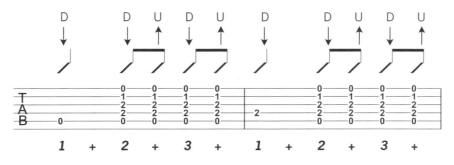

STAGE 4 BC-141—BC-149

Introduction

Stage 4 introduces some more chords—7th chords, Fmaj7 and a new way to play A— and some variations on strumming patterns. Lots of fun! Remember to add the new strumming patterns to songs you are already confident with and work on your chord changes with these new songs. Make sure you check out the Stage 4 One-Minute Changes (BC-144) for these new chords because changing between them the right way can make a huge difference to how fast you will get them under your fingers. Hopefully you are feeling a bit more confident with your rhythm playing now. Start using these new patterns as soon as you can, remembering to make sure that you are not stopping when you have to change chord. In Stage 4 you learn to 'force the changes' and it's a really important skill to develop. It will help your songs flow and sound natural so make sure you check it out and apply it!

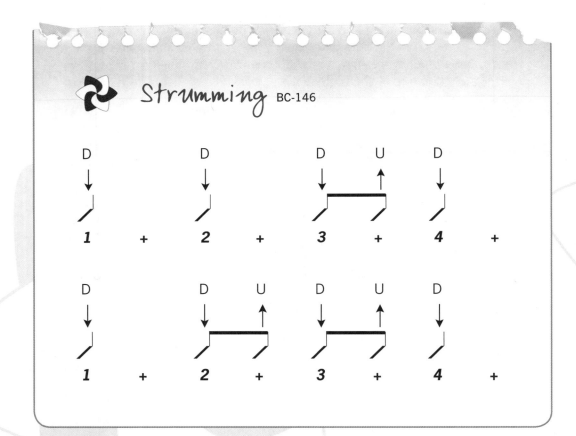

Stage 4 Chords

G7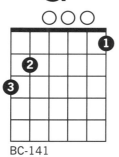
BC-141

C7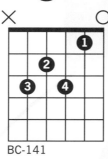
BC-141

B7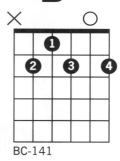
BC-141

Fmaj7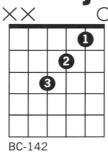
BC-142

A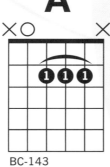
BC-143

Stage 4: Your notes

Killing Me Softly With His Song
Words by Norman Gimbel • Music by Charles Fox

Capo Fret 1

Chorus 1

    Em   Am
Strumming my pain with his fin - gers,
   D   G
Singing my life with his words,
   Em   A
Killing me softly with his song,
         D   C
Killing me softly with his song,
    G   C
Telling my whole life with his words,
   Fmaj7 Fmaj7   E   E
Killing me softly   with his song.

Verse 1

   Am   D
I heard he sang a good song,
   G   C
I heard he had a style,
   Am   D
And so I came to see him
   Em   Em
And listen for a while.
   Am   D
And there he was, this young boy,
  G   B7
A stranger to my eyes.

Chorus 2

As Chorus 1

Verse 2

I felt all flushed with fever,
Embarrassed by the crowd,
I felt he found my letters
And read each one out loud.
I prayed that he would finish,
But he just kept right on…

Chorus 3

As Chorus 2

© COPYRIGHT 1972 FOX-GIMBEL PRODUCTIONS INCORPORATED/RODALI MUSIC, USA.
HAL LEONARD CORPORATION/WARNER/CHAPPELL MUSIC NORTH AMERICA LIMITED.
ALL RIGHTS RESERVED. INTERNATIONAL COPYRIGHT SECURED.

Introduction

Reputed to have been written about 'American Pie' singer Don McLean, Roberta Flack's 1972 hit was a huge success for Haitian hip-hop heroes The Fugees in 1996 (you don't need the capo for that version).

One Chord per Bar

You play one bar for each time a chord is written in this tune. There are quite a few chords in the song so it's a great one to practise lots of chords in one go. There are many different rhythm patterns that will work with this one, so experiment.

Strumming

Many strumming patterns will work with this song, but 'old faithful' probably sounds best!

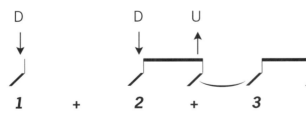

(Sittin' On) The Dock Of The Bay

Words & Music by Otis Redding & Steve Cropper

Intro | G | G | G | G |

Verse 1
```
G                      B7
Sittin' in the morning sun,
       C                       A
I'll be sittin' when the evening comes,
G                      B7
Watching the ships roll in,
       C                           A
Then I'll watch them roll a - way a - gain, yeah.
```

Chorus 1
```
       G                       E
I'm sittin' on the dock of the bay
                  G            E
Watching the tide roll a - way.
          G                    A
Just sittin' on the dock of the bay
            G   E
Wasting time. ___
```

Verse 2
I left my home in Georgia,
Headed for the 'Frisco Bay.
'Cause I've had nothing to live for,
And look like nothing's gonna come my way.

Chorus 2 As Chorus 1

Bridge
```
|G    D |C                    |
   Look like nothing's gonna change,
|G   D   |C                    |
  Everything   still remains the same.
|G    D    |C          G       |
   I can't do what ten people tell me to do,
|F             |D              |
   So I guess I'll re - main the same.
```

Verse 3
Sittin' here resting my bones
And this loneliness won't leave me alone.
Two thousand miles I've roamed
Just to make this dock my home.

Chorus 3 As Chorus 1

Coda ‖: G | G | G | E :‖ *Repeat to fade*

© COPYRIGHT 1967 EAST MEMPHIS MUSIC CORPORATION/IRVING MUSIC CORPORATION/COTILLION MUSIC INCORPORATED, USA.
RONDOR MUSIC INTERNATIONAL (ADMINISTERED IN GERMANY BY RONDOR MUSIKVERLAG GMBH)/WARNER-CHAPPELL MUSIC LIMITED.
ALL RIGHTS RESERVED. INTERNATIONAL COPYRIGHT SECURED.

Introduction

This melancholy soul classic was a hit for Otis Redding in 1967.

Pushes

This song sounds great when played simply, but when you feel totally confident with it you should try out using the 'push', where you play the chord change for a bar on the 'and' of the previous bar, which really gives a great energy to the song. You can hear it clearly in the piano part of the Otis Redding original recording (the guitar is doing it too but the piano is easier to hear).

Strumming

Don't try this one until you are feeling confident with your strumming! It's a two-bar pattern, with the chord change coming 'pushed' on the 'and' before the start of the second bar. This is going to take some practice!

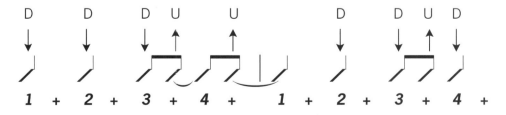

...Baby One More Time

Words & Music by Max Martin

Capo Fret 3

Verse 1
```
       Am                  E                 C
   Oh baby, baby, how was I supposed to know
      |Dm           E         |
   That something wasn't right here?
       Am                  E                 C
   Oh baby, baby, I shouldn't have let you go
      |Dm           E         |
   And now you're out of sight.
```

Pre-chorus 1
```
   Am                         E
   Show me how you want it to be,
       C                    |Dm         E      |
   Tell me baby 'cause I need to know now, just because:
```

Chorus 1
```
   Am                   E               C
      My loneliness is killing me and I,
      |Dm       E       |Am
   I must confess I still believe,   still be - lieve
                       E
   If I'm not with you I lose my mind.
           C   |Dm        E           |
   Give me a sign, hit me baby one more time.
```

Verse 2
Oh baby, baby, the reason I breathe is you:
Boy, you've got me blind.
Oh pretty baby, there's nothing that I wouldn't do,
It's not the way I planned.

Pre-chorus 2 As Pre-chorus 1

Chorus 2 As Chorus 1

Bridge
```
   Am                  E              C    |Dm   E|
      Oh baby, baby,  how was I supposed to know?
   Fmaj7            G                    Dm |Fmaj7
      Oh pretty baby, I shouldn't have let you go. ___
   G       |Am              E              C
   I must con - fess that my loneli - ness is killing me now.
      |Dm       E      |Fmaj7              G
   Don't you know I still be - lieve that you will be here,
           Fmaj7|Dm         E            |
   Just give me a sign,   hit me baby one more time.
```

Chorus 3 As Chorus 1 *(Play x2)*

© COPYRIGHT 1998 IMAGEM LONDON LIMITED.
ALL RIGHTS RESERVED. INTERNATIONAL COPYRIGHT SECURED.

Introduction

This was the song that launched Britney Spears on to the world in 1998; a brilliant bit of pop songwriting.

 ## Travis version

The Travis cover of the Britney Spears classic uses slightly different chords compared to the original and I think it works really well. To play the Travis version, place your capo at the 2nd fret, and replace each Dm chord with D. The fact that it can be stripped down to just acoustic guitar is testament to it being a great tune. Interestingly, pretty much the whole song uses the same chord progression. The only bit that changes is in the bridge; otherwise it's the same chords throughout, which should make it easy to remember.

 ## Strumming

The best pattern to use here is all down-strums (try playing a slight accent on beats 2 and 4 if you can, as shown).

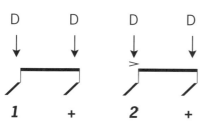

Save Tonight
Words & Music by Eagle-Eye Cherry

Chord progression throughout:
| Am Fmaj7 | C G |

Verse 1

Go and close the curtains, 'cause all we need is candlelight,
You and me and the bottle of wine,
And I'll hold you tonight.
Well we know I'm going away and how I wish, I wish it wasn't so,
So take this wine and drink with me,
Let's delay our misery.

Chorus 1

Save tonight and fight the break of dawn,
Come tomorrow, tomorrow I'll be gone.
Save tonight and fight the break of dawn,
Come tomorrow, tomorrow I'll be gone.

Verse 2

There's a log on the fire, and it burns like me for you.
Tomorrow comes with one desire: to take me away, it's true.
It ain't easy to say goodbye, darling, please don't start to cry
'Cause girl you know I've got to go
And Lord I wish it wasn't so.

Chorus 2

As Chorus 1

Solo

As above

Verse 3

Tomorrow comes to take me away,
I wish that I, that I could stay.
Girl you know I've got to go,
Oh, and Lord I wish it wasn't so.

Chorus 3

As Chorus 1 (*Repeat*)

© COPYRIGHT 1998 KOBALT MUSIC PUBLISHING LIMITED.
ALL RIGHTS RESERVED. INTERNATIONAL COPYRIGHT SECURED.

Introduction

Eagle Eye-Cherry's hit from 1998 is a great song to play, it always goes down well!

 Dynamics

The chords in this song are the same all the way through so it's very important that you get used to using dynamics to prevent it getting boring. The most obvious thing to do (probably because it works so well) is to play the verses quietly and then build up to a big chorus. This is especially important when you are playing by yourself!

Strumming

The actual rhythm pattern for this song is pretty difficult. When you're done with the whole Beginner's Course and you are happy with your strumming you might want to listen to the original song and try and match the rhythm; this pattern will work in the meantime:

   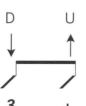 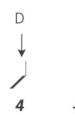

```
D           D           D   U   D
↓           ↓           ↓   ↑   ↓
1     +     2     +     3   +   4     +
```

Celebrity
Words & Music by Brad Paisley

Intro

| C | G | C | G |
| C | G Fmaj7 | C | G |

Verse 1

```
       C                     C      |G      Fmaj7  |C
Someday I'm gonna be famous,     do I have talent, well, no.
       C                             C       |G      Fmaj7  |C
These days you don't really need it     thanks to re - ality     shows.
       C                        C      |G       Fmaj7  |C
Can't wait to date a super - model,    can't wait to sue my     dad.
       C                       C     |G      Fmaj7   |C
Can't wait to wreck a Ferrari    on my way to re - hab.
```

Chorus 1

```
              |C     Fmaj7 |G               |C    Fmaj7 |G
'Cause when you're a cele - bri - ty, it's adios re - a - li - ty.
                          Am                    Fmaj7
You can act just like a fool and people think you're cool
                G     G
Just 'cause you're on T. - V.
          |C    Fmaj7 |G              |C    Fmaj7 |G
I can throw a ma - jor   fit when my latte isn't  just how I like it.
                      Am                    Fmaj7
They say I've gone in - sane, I'll blame it on the fame
                  G                     (C)
And the pressures that go with being a celebrity.
```

Link 1

| C | G Fmaj7 | C | G |

Verse 2

I'll get to cry to Barbara Walters when things don't go my way.
I'll get community service no matter which law I break.
I'll make the supermarket tabloids, they'll write some awful stuff.
But the more they run my name down, the more my price goes up.

Chorus 2

'Cause when you're a celebrity, it's adios reality.
No matter what you do, people think you're cool
Just 'cause you're on T.V.
I can fall in and out of love, have marriages that barely last a month.
When they go down the drain, I'll blame it on the fame
And say it's just so tough being a celebrity.

Link 2

| C | G Fmaj7 | C | G |

© COPYRIGHT 2003 EMI MUSIC PUBLISHING LIMITED/WORDS & MUSIC COPYRIGHT ADMINISTRATION, USA.
ALL RIGHTS RESERVED. INTERNATIONAL COPYRIGHT SECURED.

| | (G)   Am   Fmaj7
| **Bridge** | So let's hitch up the wagons and head out West
| | C   G
| | To the land of fun in the sun.
| | Am   Fmaj7
| | We'll be a real-world bachelor, jackass millionaires.
| | C   G   G
| | Hey, hey, Hollywood,   here we come.

Link 3 | C | G   Fmaj7 | C | Fmaj7 G |

Chorus 3 Yeah when you're a celebrity, it's adios reality
No matter what you do, people think you're cool
Just 'cause your on T.V. being a celebrity.
Yeah, celebrity.

Outro | C | G | C | G |
             | C | G   Fmaj7 | C |

Introduction

Brad Paisley's sly comment on reality-show driven nanostars.
Like most Paisley songs, it features astounding country picking licks.

Strumming

As you progress with your rhythm playing you should try and imitate songs and rhythms that you hear. The rhythm at the start of this song is quite interesting and is a good one to try. You should already have the skills to play it; try getting the rhythm right just by listening. This is a very valuable challenge if you choose to accept it!

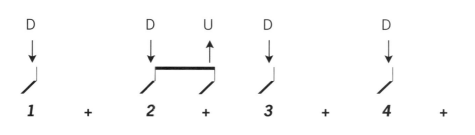

Back To December
Words & Music by Taylor Swift

Capo Fret 2

Verse 1

    C
I'm so glad you made time to see me,
    Am
How's life? Tell me, how's your family?
Fmaj7 | **C**   **G** |
I haven't seen them in a while.

    C
You've been good, busier than ever,
    Am
We small talk, work and the weather,
Fmaj7 | **C**   **G** |
Your guard is up and I know why.

Pre-chorus 1

|**Am**   **G**
Because the last time you saw me,
|**C**   **Fmaj7**
It still burned in the back of your mind.
        |**Am**   **G** |**Fmaj7**
You gave me roses and I left them there to die.

Chorus 1

    C
So this is me swallowing my pride,
              Em   **Fmaj7**
Standing in front of you saying I'm sorry for that night,
   |**C**   **G** |
And I go back to December all the time.
    C
It turns out freedom ain't nothing but missing you,
Em   **Fmaj7**
Wishing I'd realised what I had when you were mine.
  |**C**   **G** |**Fmaj7**
I go back to December, turn around and make it all right,
  |**Am**   **G** | (2° Change my own mind)
I go back to December all the time.

Link 1

‖: **C** | **Am** **Fmaj7** :‖

Verse 2

These days I haven't been sleeping,
Staying up, playing back myself leaving
When your birthday passed and I didn't call.
Then I think about summer, all the beautiful times
I watched you laughing from the passenger side
And realised I loved you in the fall.

Pre-chorus 2

And then the cold came, the dark days, when fear crept into my mind.
You gave me all your love and all I gave you was goodbye.

Chorus 2

As Chorus 1

© COPYRIGHT 2010 TAYLOR SWIFT MUSIC/SONY/ATV TREE PUBLISHING, USA.
SONY/ATV MUSIC PUBLISHING.
ALL RIGHTS RESERVED. INTERNATIONAL COPYRIGHT SECURED.

Link 2

|: C | Am Fmaj7 :|

Bridge

(Fmaj7) |Am   Fmaj7
I miss your tan skin, your sweet smile,
|C   G
So good to me, so right.
          |Am   Fmaj7 |C
And how you held me in your arms that September night,
              G |
The first time you ever saw me cry.
Am
    Maybe this is wishful thinking,
Fmaj7
    Probably mindless dreaming,
C   G
    But if we loved again, I swear I'd love you right.
   |Am   G |Fmaj7
I'd go back in time and change it, but I can't.
   |Am   G |Fmaj7
So if the chain is on your door I under - stand.

Chorus 3   As Chorus 1

Outro
|C   G |Fmaj7
I go back to December, turn around and make it all right,
|Am   G |Fmaj7
I go back to December, turn around and change my own mind,
|Am   G |C |Am Fmaj7|
I go back to December all the time,
        C |Am Fmaj7|
All the time.

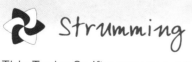

This Taylor Swift song uses a type of strumming that we don't cover in the Beginner's Course; here it is has an eighth-note two-bar pattern; you just have to count it faster. Listen carefully to the original record! Listening is ALWAYS the answer to the question: "how does it go?"

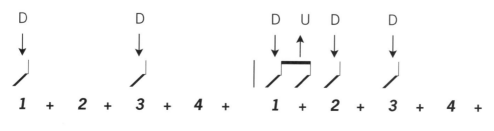

Black

Words by Eddie Vedder • Music by Stone Gossard

Verse 1

E   A   E   A
Sheets of empty canvas, untouched sheets of clay.
          E   A   E   E
Her legs spread out be - fore me as her body was there.
E   A   E   A
All five ho - rizons revolved a - round the sun, I see earth through the sun.
E   A   E   E
Now the air I tasted and breathed has taken a turn.

Chorus 1

(E) C   C   Em   Em
Ooh,__ and all I taught her was every - thing.
      C   C   Em   Em
Ooh,__ I know she gave me all that she wore.
          D
And now my bitter hands shake
      C   Em
Be - neath the clouds of what was every - thing.
    D   C   Em
All the pictures have all been washed in black, tattooed every day.

Verse 2

I take a walk outside, I'm surrounded by some kids at play.
I can feel their laughter, so what do I say?

Chorus 2

(E) C   C   Em   Em
Oh, hot and twisted thoughts that spin 'round my head, I'm spinning,
     C   C   Em   Em
Oh, I'm spinning, how quick the sun can drop a - way.
       D   C   Em
And now my bitter hands they're on broken glass of what was every day.
    D   C   Em
All the pictures have all been washed in black, tattooed every day.
    D   C
All the love gone bad turned my world to black,
        D   C   Em D   C
Tattooed all I see, all that I am, all I'll be,__ yeah.
Em   D   C
Uh huh, uh huh, ooh.

Outro

Em
I know someday you'll have a beautiful life,
D   C
I know you'll be a star in somebody else's sky,
      Em   D   C   Em D C
But why, why, why can't it be, can't it be mine?____

© COPYRIGHT 1991 WRITE TREATAGE MUSIC/INNOCENT BYSTANDER MUSIC, USA.
UNIVERSAL MUSIC PUBLISHING LIMITED/KOBALT MUSIC PUBLISHING LIMITED.
ALL RIGHTS RESERVED. INTERNATIONAL COPYRIGHT SECURED.

Introduction

'Black' featured on Pearl Jam's debut album *Ten* in 1991.

Singing and Playing

This song is a hard one to sing and play at the same time because of the way Pearl Jam vocalist Eddie Vedder phrases the words. If you want to try singing and playing this one it's going to take a lot of listening to the original (which is never a bad thing!). Get the strumming pattern below nice and solid—so you can play it without thinking about it—and then try singing over the top.

Strumming

The strumming in this is pretty complicated and it changes a lot during the song, so best to keep it simple and make it sound good until you feel confident enough to try experimenting yourself!

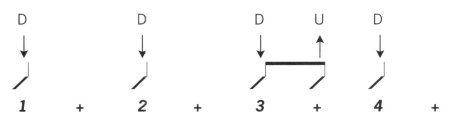

Little Lion Man
Words & Music by Mumford & Sons

Capo Fret 5

Intro

‖: Am | Am | C | C :‖

Verse 1

Am
Weep for yourself, my man,
     Am   **C**   **C**
You'll never be what is in your heart.
Am
Weep little lion man,
     Am   **C**   **C**
You're not as brave as you were at the start.
G
Rate yourself and rake yourself,
Fmaj7   **C**   **C**
Take all the courage you have   left.
     G
You wasted on fixing all the
Fmaj7   **C**   **C**
Problems that you made in your own   head.

Chorus 1

|Am   Fmaj7|C
But it was not your fault but mine,
|Am   Fmaj7|C
And it was your heart on the line.
|Am   Fmaj7|C
I really ******** it up this time,
          G   **G**
Didn't I, my dear?

Didn't I, my?

Link 1

‖: Am | Am | C | C :‖

Verse 2

Tremble for yourself, my man,
You know that you have seen this all before.
Tremble little lion man,
You'll never settle any of your scores.
Your grace is wasted in your face,
Your boldness stands alone among the wreck.
Now learn from your mother or else
Spend your days biting your own neck.

© COPYRIGHT 2009 UNIVERSAL MUSIC PUBLISHING LIMITED.
ALL RIGHTS RESERVED. INTERNATIONAL COPYRIGHT SECURED.

Chorus 2	As Chorus 1
Chorus 3	As Chorus 1
Interlude	‖: Am | Am | C | C :‖ C | C |
	| Fmaj7 | Fmaj7 | G | C | Fmaj7 | Fmaj7 ‖
	‖: G | C | Fmaj7 | Fmaj7 :‖ *Play x6*
	Ah._____
Chorus 4	But it was not your fault but mine,
	And it was your heart on the line.
	I really ******* it up this time,
	Didn't I, my dear?
	But it was not your fault but mine,
	And it was your heart on the line.
	I really ******* it up this time,
	Didn't I, my dear?
	Didn't I, my dear?

 ## Introduction

The breakthrough single for Mumford & Sons in 2009. The original song uses an alternate tuning for the guitar, but the song works really well with these more straightforward chord shapes.

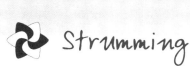 ## Strumming

This song has been simplified a lot, but will still sound pretty close to the original with a little practice. The main pain here is the strumming which is a very fast up-strum, almost like it's skipping! This is beyond many beginner players, but if you are really feeling confident with your rhythm skills then by all means try it out.

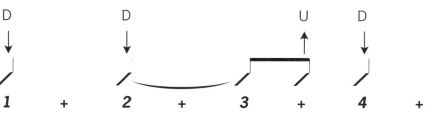

Live Forever
Words & Music by Noel Gallagher

Verse 1
```
       G              D
Maybe I don't really want to know
                Am
How your garden grows,
| C         D     |
 I just want to fly.
G             D
Lately, did you ever feel the pain
             Am
In the morning rain
 | C          D      |
As it soaks you to the bone.
```

Chorus 1
```
Em              D                              Am
 Maybe I just want to fly, I want to live, I don't want to die,
  |  C          D        |   Em
Maybe I just want to breathe, maybe I just don't be - lieve.
              D
Maybe you're the same as me,
            Am                              Fmaj7  Fmaj7
We see things they'll never see, you and I are gonna live for - ever.
```

Verse 2
I said maybe I don't really want to know
How your garden grows,
I just want to fly.
Lately, did you ever feel the pain
In the morning rain
As it soaks you to the bone.

Chorus 2
Maybe I will never be all the things I want to be,
But now is not the time to cry, now's the time to find out why
I think you're the same as me,
We see things they'll never see, you and I are gonna live forever.

Guitar solo — Chords as Verse 1 and Chorus 1

Verse 3 — As Verse 1

Chorus 3 — As Chorus 1

Outro
```
 ||: Am              Fmaj7    :||  Play x6
     Gonna live for - ever.
```

© COPYRIGHT 1994 CREATION SONGS LIMITED/OASIS MUSIC (GB).
SONY/ATV MUSIC PUBLISHING.
ALL RIGHTS RESERVED. INTERNATIONAL COPYRIGHT SECURED.

Introduction

One of Oasis' most enduring songs. Originally released as a single from their debut album *Definitely Maybe* in 1994, it has been played live at virtually every Oasis gig since.

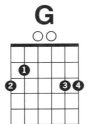

The 'Big' G BC-181

This is a great song to get the big four finger G chord going—it's very much part of the Oasis sound. Although it makes some of the chord changes a little harder, it produces a much bigger sound than the standard G shape and is very commonly used in rock and pop.

 ## Strumming

This one is really a sixteenth-note pattern but I'm showing it here as eighth-notes so you can get started with it. It's not tricky!

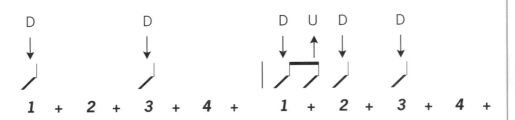

I Want To Hold Your Hand
Words & Music by John Lennon & Paul McCartney

Intro
| C D | D | C D | D | C D | D | D | |

Verse 1
(D)   G   D
Oh yeah, I'll tell you something,
Em   B7
I think you'll understand.
    G   D
When I say that something,
Em   B7
I wanna hold your hand.

Chorus 1
| C   D | G Em | C   D | G |
   I wanna hold your hand,___   I wanna hold your hand.

Verse 2
Oh please say to me
You'll let me be your man.
And please say to me
You'll let me hold your hand.

Chorus 2   As Chorus 1

Middle 1
Dm   G   C   Am
And when I touch you I feel happy inside.
Dm   G
It's such a feeling
       C |D C |D C |D |D |
That my love I can't hide, I can't hide, I can't hide.

Verse 3
Yeah, you got that something,
I think you'll understand.
When I say that something,
I wanna hold your hand.

Chorus 3   As Chorus 2

Middle 2   As Middle 1

Verse 4   As Verse 3

Chorus 4
| C   D | G Em |
   I wanna hold your hand,___
| C   D | B7 |
   I wanna hold your hand,
| C   D | C | G |
   I wanna hold your hand.

© COPYRIGHT 1963 SONY/ATV MUSIC PUBLISHING.
ALL RIGHTS RESERVED. INTERNATIONAL COPYRIGHT SECURED.

Introduction

This was the song that launched Beatlemania in the U.S.A. after the Fab Four performed on *The Ed Sullivan Show* in 1963.

Single Note runs

If you feel confident with the chords you should have a go at working out the little single note runs between the chords. They are all on the lowest two strings and are not hard to figure out.

Strumming

Keeping it really simple (like the Beatles did) sounds best for this one!

  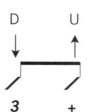 

```
D           D           D    U    D
↓           ↓           ↓    ↑    ↓

1     +     2     +     3    +    4     +
```

STAGE 5 BC-151—BC-159

Introduction

We've now looked at most of the open position 7th chords, which means you can play a blues in many different keys, and so many of the songs in this stage are blues-based. They are lots of fun and as you learn more blues techniques you will be able to apply them to these songs too, but it's best to start with strumming through them to get the groove solid.

The best way to learn the grooves in blues is to listen. It's just like a language: you have to listen to it to know how it should sound. Blues is an aural tradition—it is passed down to the next generation by people listening—and so you can't learn the blues by reading or study. If you are not familiar with these artists then go and buy a few albums and get the sounds, songs and feel into your head!

As ever, keep going with your One-Minute Changes (BC-154) and also have a look at Air Changes (BC-153).

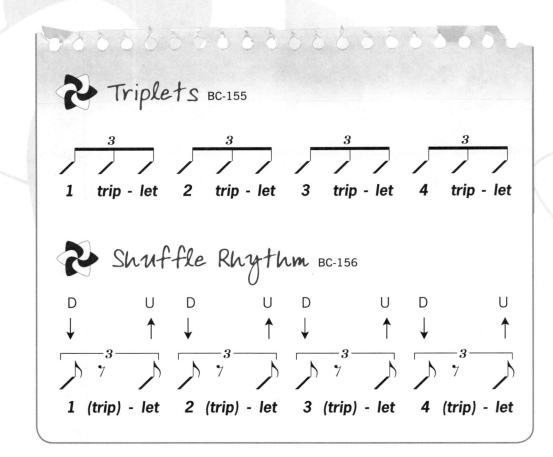

Stage 5 Chords

A7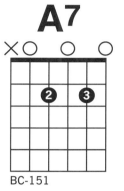

D7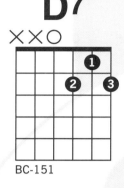

E7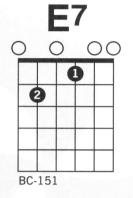

BC-151   BC-151   BC-151

Stage 5: Your notes

Before You Accuse Me (Take A Look At Yourself)
Words & Music by Ellas McDaniel

12-bar blues chord progression throughout:

E	A	E	E
A	A	E	E
B7	A	E	B7

Chorus 1

    E   A   E   E
Be - fore you accuse me, take a look at your - self.
    A   A   E   E
Be - fore you accuse me, take a look at your - self.
        B7
You say I'm spending my money on other women,
A   E   B7
    You're taking money from someone else.

Verse 1

    E   A   E   E
I called your mama 'bout three or four nights a - go.
    A   A   E   E
I called your mama 'bout three or four nights a - go.
        B7   A   E   B7
Well your mama said, "Son, don't call my daughter no more."

Chorus 2 As Chorus 1

Guitar solo 1 As Verse chords

Verse 2

Come on back home baby, try my love one more time.
Come on back home baby, try my love one more time.
You know if things don't go to suit you, I think I'll lose my mind.

Chorus 3 As Chorus 1

Guitar solo 2 As Verse chords

© COPYRIGHT 1957 EMI LONGITUDE MUSIC, USA.
EMI MUSIC PUBLISHING LIMITED.
ALL RIGHTS RESERVED. INTERNATIONAL COPYRIGHT SECURED.

Introduction

You might know this song from Eric Clapton's multi-Grammy Award winning *Unplugged* album, but the Bo Diddley original and Creedence Clearwater Revival version should definitely be investigated.

Getting the Right Feel

The trick, if there is one, for getting a good blues feel is listening. A good idea is to pick a version of the song (maybe the Eric Clapton or Creedence Clearwater Revival one) and really try and cop the groove and the feel of it. It's very hard to explain, but when you really listen and try to copy the feel of a track it will give you that extra magic that makes it sound like the recording. It's something that can't be written down; you will only ever really get it by listening. Often the wisest people (and best players) are those that listen the most.

Strumming

Further through the course you will learn to play a 12-Bar Blues-style shuffle rhythm, which will sound great in this song and the other blues tunes in this stage. For now have a go at getting through the songs with any rhythm you feel comfortable with. The cool thing with playing the blues is that a lot is down to interpretation. There are a billion versions of this song, so you can experiment with it too! A good way to start is just by playing eighth-notes while trying to get a bit of the shuffle feel.

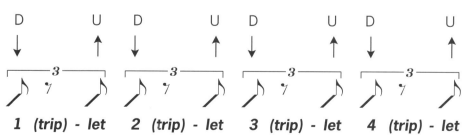

Folsom Prison Blues
Words & Music by Johnny Cash

Capo Fret 1

Intro	| B7 | B7 | E | E |

Verse 1

    E   E   E   E
I hear the train a-comin' it's rollin' round the bend,
      E   E   E   E
And I ain't seen the sunshine since, I don't know when.
  A   A   A   A   E   E   E
I'm stuck in Folsom Prison, and time keeps draggin' on.
      B7   B7 B7   B7   E   E
But that train keeps rollin' on down to San An - tone.

Verse 2

When I was just a baby, my mama told me
"Son, always be a good boy, don't ever play with guns."
But I shot a man in Reno just to watch him die.
When I hear that whistle blowin' I hang my head and cry.

Guitar solo 1

| E	| E	| E	| E	|
| E	| E	| E	| E	|
| A	| A	| A	| A	|
| E	| E	| E	| E	|
| B7	| B7	| B7	| B7	| E | E |

Verse 3

I bet there's rich folks eatin' in a fancy dining car.
They're probably drinkin' coffee and smokin' big cigars.
Well I know I had it comin', I know I can't be free,
But those people keep a-movin' and that's what tortures me.

Guitar solo 2   As Solo 1 chords

Verse 4

Well if they freed me from this prison, if that railroad train was mine,
I bet I'd move it on a little farther down the line,
Far from Folsom Prison, that's where I want to stay,
And I'd let that lonesome whistle blow my blues away.

Outro | B7 | B7 | E | E |

© COPYRIGHT 1956 HILL & RANGE SONGS INCORPORATED/CHAPPELL & COMPANY INCORPORATED, USA.
CARLIN MUSIC CORPORATION.
ALL RIGHTS RESERVED. INTERNATIONAL COPYRIGHT SECURED.

Introduction

Johnny Cash originally released this as a single in 1955, imagining life as a prisoner. However, the song's place in music history was sealed when he performed at the actual Folsom Prison in 1968 for the benefit of the inmates, capturing the gig on his classic live LP *At Folsom Prison*.

 ## Open String Chord Changes

When you have an up-stroke on the 'and' after 4 it can seem impossible to get the chord changes fast enough. The truth is that most times (but not ALL the time!) players start changing the chord early and that last strum in the bar ends up as just open strings. It would seem at first like a bad idea—like you are cheating—but if you listen out for it on recordings you will hear it often.

More 'boom chick-a boom chick-a'

This song has a great 'train' rhythm ('boom chick-a boom chick-a') on the acoustic guitar. You have to listen under the lead guitar to hear it clearly. The down-strums on beats 1 and 3 are light, and mainly focused on the thick strings; the down-strums on beats 2 and 4 are quite heavy on all the strings, and the up-stokes following are back to normal volume. To get grooves like this right is very hard and takes lots of practice—but you'll get it by listening to the track a lot. You'll never get it right if you are not sure what it's supposed to sound like!

 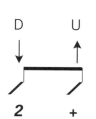  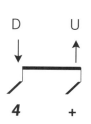

Sweet Little Angel
Words & Music by B.B. King & J. Taub

Capo Fret 6

12-bar blues chord progression thoughout:

G7	C7	G7	G7
C7	C7	G7	G7
D7	C7	G7	D7

Intro

G7	C7	G7	G7
C7	C7	G7	G7
D7	C7	G7	D7

Verse 1

G7   C7
I've got a sweet little angel,
  G7   G7
I love the way she spreads her wings
              C7   C7
Yeah, I've got a sweet little angel,
         G7   G7
I love the way she spreads her wings.
               D7   C7
Yes, when she spreads her wings around me,
   G7   D7
I gets joy and every - thing.

Verse 2

Lord, if my baby should quit me,
I do believe I would die.
Yes, if my, my baby should quit me,
I do believe I would die.
Yes, if you don't love me little angel,
Please tell me the reason why.

Guitar solo

As Verse chords

Verse 3

Yes, I asked my baby for a nickel
And she gave me a twenty dollar bill.
Yes, I asked my baby for a nickel
And she gave me a twenty dollar bill.
Yes, you know I ask her to let's go out and have a good time,
And she bought me a Cadillac Seville.

© COPYRIGHT CAREERS-BMG MUSIC PUBLISHING INCORPORATED, USA.
UNIVERSAL MUSIC PUBLISHING MGB LIMITED.
ALL RIGHTS RESERVED. INTERNATIONAL COPYRIGHT SECURED.

Introduction

This B.B. King blues—also known as 'Black Angel Blues'—has been recorded by numerous artists from Jeff Beck to Big Mama Thornton. B.B. King recorded it several times, including on live performances with James Brown.

Listen To the Drums!

The B.B. King version of this song on *Live At The Regal* is the one that moves me: it's just perfect. Interestingly, B.B. doesn't play rhythm, he just plays lead guitar, so the main groove is played here on the piano, and you will clearly hear the triplet feel used in the whole song. Counting along "1 trip-let, 2 trip-let, 3 trip-let, 4 trip-let" will help you cop the feel. If you have trouble hearing the triplets, from about 3:30 in the track the drummer is hitting his ride cymbal in the left speaker on each note in the triplet. That should help! Then try the strumming suggested below.

Strumming

A good feel for this tune can be to play a whole bar of triplets with all down-strums. Count along as you play to start off with; it can help a lot to accent the 1, 2, 3 and 4, just make them a touch louder. With a bit of practice you'll be there in no time!

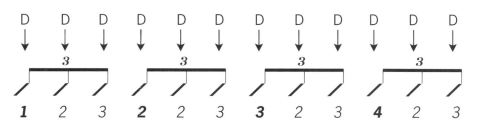

Crossroads
by Robert Johnson

12-Bar blues chord progression:

A7	A7	A7	A7
D7	D7	A7	A7
E7	D7	A7	A7

Verse 1

      A7
I went down to the crossroads,
D7   **A7**   **A7**
  Fell down on my knees.
D7   **D7**
Down to the crossroads,
             A7   **A7**
Fell down on my knees.
E7
  Asked the Lord above for mercy,
D7   **A7**   **A7**
  Take me if you please.

Verse 2

I went down to the crossroads,
Tried to flag a ride.
Down to the crossroads,
Tried to flag a ride.
Nobody seemed to know me,
Everybody passed me by.

Verse 3

Well I'm going down to Rosedale,
Take my rider by my side.
Going down to Rosedale,
Take my rider by my side.
We can still barrel-house, baby,
On the riverside.

Verse 4   As Verse 3

Verse 5

You can run, you can run,
Tell my friend Boy Willy Brown.
Run, you can run,
Tell my friend Boy Willy Brown,
That I'm standing at the crossroads,
Believe I'm sinking down.

© COPYRIGHT 2011 DORSEY BROTHERS MUSIC LIMITED.
ALL RIGHTS RESERVED. INTERNATIONAL COPYRIGHT SECURED.

Introduction

This is one of the quintessential blues lyrics, interpreted in many ways by the great blues artists.

Original Versions

There are many hundred of versions of this song. The best known is Cream's (with Eric Clapton on guitar) but this is an old song, originally credited to Robert Johnson. The song has a very distinctive riff not covered here but worth checking out a little later.

Strumming

This one takes the 12-Bar Shuffle you will learn in BC-183, but a regular shuffle rhythm will sound groovy too, and makes a great second guitar part if you jam with someone playing the 12-Bar Shuffle.

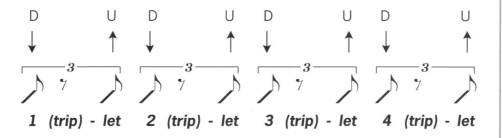

Evil (Is Going On)
Words & Music by Willie Dixon

12-bar blues chord progression throughout:

G7	G7	G7	G7
C7	C7	G7	G7
D7	C7	G7	G7 D7

Verse 1

   G7   G7
If you're a long way from home, can't sleep at night,
   G7   G7
Grab your telephone, something just ain't right.
     C7   C7   G7   G7
That's evil. Evil is going on wrong.
    D7   C7
I am warning you brother,
                         G7 | G7 D7 |
You better watch your happy home.

Verse 2

Well, long way from home and can't sleep at all,
You know another mule is kickin' in your stall.
That's evil. Evil is going on wrong.
I am warning you brother,
You better watch your happy home.

Verse 3

Well, if you call her on the telephone,
And she answers awful slow
Grab the first thing smoking if you have to hobo,
That's evil. Evil is going on wrong.
I am warning you brother,
You better watch your happy home.

Verse 4

If you make it to your house, knock on the front door,
Run around to the back, you'll catch him just before he goes.
That's evil. Evil is going on.
I am warning you brother,
You better watch your happy home.

© COPYRIGHT 1960, 1988 HOOCHIE COOCHIE MUSIC, USA.
BUG MUSIC LIMITED.
ALL RIGHTS RESERVED. INTERNATIONAL COPYRIGHT SECURED.

Introduction

Howlin' Wolf's tale of domestic vigilence from 1954.

Listen to the drummer!

Listening to the drums will help you get the right rhythm for this song. If you're playing along make sure that you are doing your strums right with the drums: that way you will know you have the rhythm solid. Also, listen to the way that the guitar sits with the other instruments in the band—the bass, piano, harmonica and the drums— to create the groove.

Strumming

A really cool rhythm pattern for this blues is just to play a down-strum on beat 1 and an up-strum on the 'and' after 2. Count it out really slow and play along with your own count until it clicks, and then try to play the rhythm pattern with the chord changes as well.

D							
↓		U					
		↑					
1	+	2	+	3	+	4	+

Mary Had A Little Lamb
Words & Music by Buddy Guy

Intro

| 𝄆 E7 | E7 | E7 | E7 |
| A7 | A7 | E7 | E7 |
| B7 | A7 | E7 | E7 | 𝄇

Verse 1

N.C.   A7
Mary had a little lamb,
 A7   E7
 Its fleece was white as snow, yeah.
E7   B7
 Everywhere the child went,
A7   E7 E7
 The little lamb was sure to go, yeah.

Verse 2

He followed her to school one day
And broke the teacher's rule.
What a time did they have,
That day at school.

Guitar solo

| 𝄆 A7 | A7 | E7 | E7 |
| B7 | A7 | E7 | E7 | 𝄇 Play x3

Verse 3

Tisket, tasket, baby,
A green and yellow basket.
Sent a letter to my baby,
On my way I passed it.

Outro

E7	E7	E7	E7
A7	A7	E7	E7
B7	A7	E7	E7

© COPYRIGHT 1983 MIC SHAU MUSIC.
BUG MUSIC LIMITED.
ALL RIGHTS RESERVED. INTERNATIONAL COPYRIGHT SECURED.

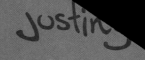

 ## Introduction

'Mary Had A Little Lamb' was written by Buddy Guy, but became a staple of Texan bluesman Stevie Ray Vaughan's live set. Check it out on Vaughan's *Texas Flood* album (1983). P ease note—if you want to play along with SRV you'll need to tune your guitar down a semitone (Use your tuner: E♭, A♭, D♭, G♭, B♭, E♭).

 ## Write the chords out yourself!

If you come across a song and the sequence of chords is not clear—try writing it out yourself and count along with the music to check how many bars each chord is played for. You will learn a whole lot in the process and when you get used to doing it you will find using chord books a lot easier, as well. Often it makes it a lot easier to remember the chords too, because it helps the pattern become clear. It takes a little bit of work…but you see, anything worth doing takes a little effort!

 ## Strumming

The rhythm playing in the Stevie Ray Vaughan version of this tune is very complex, but it will sound great with a simple shuffle too, and it's a fun one to get people to sing along, because everyone knows the words!

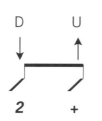

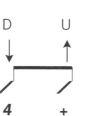

Down Slow
by James B. Oden

12-bar blues chord progression throughout:

G7	C7	G7	G7
C7	C7	G7	G7
D7	C7	G7 C7	G7 D7

Verse 1

G7   C7   G7   G7
   I have had my fun   if I   don't get well no more.
C7   C7   G7   G7
I have had my fun   if I don't   get well no more.
D7   C7 |G7   C7 | G7 D7|
My, my health is failing,   and now I'm going down slow.

Verse 2

G7   C7   G7   G7
   If you see my mother,   tell her the shape I'm in.
C7   C7   G7   G7
If, if you see my mother, tell her the shape I'm in.
D7   C7 |G7
Tell her to pray for me,   forgive me for all my sins
                          C7 |G7   D7|
And I've got a lot of 'em, hope to have some more before the night's over.

Guitar solo   As Verse chords

Verse 3

G7   C7   G7   G7
   Tell her don't send no doctor,   doctor can't do no good.
C7   C7   G7   G7
Tell her, tell her don't send no doctor, doctor can't do no good.
D7   C7 |G7
 'Cause I play so hard,   I'd do the same damn thing again if I could.
   C7 | G7   D7 |
Oh yeah,   oh.

© COPYRIGHT 1943 WABASH MUSIC COMPANY/LEEDS MUSIC CORPORATION. ASSIGNED TO
MCA MUSIC (A DIVISION OF MUSIC CORPORATION OF AMERICA), USA.
UNIVERSAL/MCA MUSIC LIMITED.
RIGHTS RESERVED. INTERNATIONAL COPYRIGHT SECURED.

Introduction

This blues standard has been recorded by many major blues artists. A good place to start is Jimmy Witherspoon and Robben Ford *Live From The Monteray Jazz Festival* from 1972.

 ## Stick to the Form

On thing that often confuses people when reading a chord book like this is the lyric spacing. It's very important to realize that nearly all songs have a set chord progression which you have to stick to. To help out we have put the chord sequence into bars at the top of the page. If you look at verse 1 and verse 2 they look like they might be different because of the way the chords are spaced out, but they are not—they are played exactly the same, it's just some of the words are sung faster and so they need more page space.

 ## Strumming

This is a ballad and really simple strumming works best. As your rhythm skills develop you will be able to add in more complex stuff, but it's a great one to just play nice, easy four down-strums to a bar. With the right intent, that will have more depth than playing lots of notes just for the sake of it.

D ↓	D ↓	D ↓	D ↓
1 trip - let	2 trip - let	3 trip - let	4 trip - let

I Saw Her Standing There
Words & Music by John Lennon & Paul McCartney

Intro | E7 | E7 | E7 | E7 |

Verse 1
                       E7   E7
Well, she was just seventeen,
    A7   E7
You know what I mean,
            E7   E7   B7
And the way she looked was way beyond com - pare.
         E   E7   A   C
So how could I dance with another, Oh,
       E7   B7   E7   E7
When I saw her standing there.

Verse 2
Well, she looked at me,
And I, I could see,
That before too long, I'd fall in love with her.
She wouldn't dance with another, oh,
When I saw her standing there.

Bridge 1
      A7   A7   A7   A7
Well, my heart went boom, when I crossed that room,
  A7   A7   B7   B7   A7 A7
And I held her hand in mine. _____

Verse 3
Well, we danced through the night,
And we held each other tight,
And before too long I fell in love with her.
Now I'll never dance with another,
Oh, when I saw her standing there.

Solo | E7 | E7 | E7 | E7 | E7 | E7 |
       | B7 | B7 | E7 | E7 | A7 | A7 |
       | E7 | B7 | E7 | E7 |

Bridge 2 As Bridge 1

Verse 4
Oh, we danced through the night,
And we held each other tight,
And before too long I fell in love with her.
Now I'll never dance with another, oh,
Since I saw her standing there,
Oh, since I saw her standing there,
Yeah, well since I saw her standing there.

© COPYRIGHT 1963 SONY/ATV MUSIC PUBLISHING.
ALL RIGHTS RESERVED. INTERNATIONAL COPYRIGHT SECURED.

Introduction
This song kicked off the first Beatles LP *Please Please Me* in 1963.

Strumming more than one Pattern

Many songs have a different strumming pattern for the verses and the choruses. This adds dynamics and lifts the chorus up. For this song you can go to straight 8s (pumping all down-strums on 1 + 2 + 3 + 4 +) and it will sound grand. You can also get some 12-Bar Blues Shuffle action going on this one too—and maybe even using some of the variations taught later in Stage 9!

Strumming

This pattern might take you a little while to master, but listen to the original Beatles record, play along and you'll soon crack the groove.

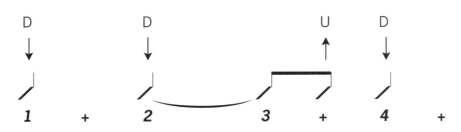

Mrs. Robinson
Words & Music by Paul Simon

Capo Fret 2

Intro

|: E | E | E | E :|

E	E	E	E	E7

Di di di di di di di di di di di di di

| A7 | A7 | A7 | A7 |

Doo doo doo doo doo doo doo doo doo

| D7 | G | C | Am | Am | E | E | D7 |

Di di di di di di di di di di di di di.

Chorus 1

D7   G   Em
  And here's to you, Mrs. Robinson
G   Em   C   C   D   D
Jesus loves you more than you will know   (wo, wo, wo.)
(D)   G   Em
  God bless you please, Mrs. Robinson,
G   Em   C   C
Heaven holds a place for those who pray
        Am Am   E | E | E | E |
(Hey, hey, hey,   hey, hey, hey.)

Verse 1

   E   E   E   E   E7
We'd like to know a little bit a - bout you for our files,
   A7   A7   A7   A7
We'd like to help you learn to help your - self.
D7   G | C G | Am   Am
  Look around you, all you see are sympathetic eyes.
E7   E7   D7   D7
  Stroll around the grounds un - til you feel at home.

Chorus 2   As Chorus 1

Verse 2

Hide it in a hiding place where no one ever goes,
Put it in your pantry with your cupcakes.
It's a little secret, just the Robinsons' affair.
Most of all, you've got to hide it from the kids.

Chorus 3   As Chorus 2

Verse 3

Sitting on a sofa on a Sunday afternoon,
Going to the candidates' debate.
Laugh about it, shout about it
When you've got to choose.
Every way you look at it, you lose.

Chorus 4

Where have you gone, Joe DiMaggio?
A nation turns its lonely eyes to you (woo, woo, woo)
What's that you say, Mrs. Robinson?
Joltin' Joe has left and gone away
(Hey, hey, hey, hey, hey, hey.)

© COPYRIGHT 1968, 1970 PAUL SIMON (BMI).
ALL RIGHTS RESERVED. INTERNATIONAL COPYRIGHT SECURED.

Introduction

Featured on the soundtrack to *The Graduate* (1968), this Simon & Garfunkel song is a 1960s classic. The Lemonheads' grunged-up version from 1992 is worth hearing, too.

Tap your foot!

This song has many complex guitar parts and so it can seem hard to jam along with this track. The secret is to make sure you are confident with where the beat is. Get your foot tapping along with it, without trying to play guitar. Once you can do that you shouldn't have too much hassle getting the guitar part in sync (that is, if you have been practising tapping your foot while working on your strumming, which you have, right?!).

Strumming

To get this strumming pattern sounding good, it's best to accent beat 1 a bit—having no strum on the 'and' before 2 makes beat 1 stand out a little anyhow, but just give it a little more volume than the rest and it will sound cool.

D		D	U	D	U	D	U
↓		↓	↑	↓	↑	↓	↑
1	+	2	+	3	+	4	+

That'll Be The Day
Words & Music by Buddy Holly, Norman Petty & Jerry Allison

Chorus 1

        D   D
Well, that'll be the day when you say goodbye
        A   A
Yes, that'll be the day when you make me cry
        D   D
You say you're gonna leave, you know it's a lie
      | A (N.C.) | E7   A |
'Cause that'll be the day when I die.

Verse 1

                       D   A
Well, you give me all your lovin' and your   turtle dovin'
            D   A
All your hugs and kisses and your   money too
       D
Well,   you know you love me baby,
A
   Still you tell me, maybe,
B7   E7
That some day, well, I'll be through.

Chorus 2   As Chorus 1

Guitar solo

A	A	A	A
D	D	A	A
E7	D	A	E7

Chorus 3   As Chorus 1

Verse 2

Well, when Cupid shot his dart he shot it at your heart
So if we ever part then I'll leave you
You sit and hold me and you tell me boldly
That some day, well, I'll be blue.

Chorus 4   As Chorus 1

Outro

          D   D
Well, that'll be the day,   woo hoo,
A   A
That'll be the day,   woo hoo,
D   D
That'll be the day,   woo hoo,
A
That'll be the day.

© COPYRIGHT 1957 MPL COMMUNICATIONS INCORPORATED, USA.
PEERMUSIC (UK) LIMITED.
ALL RIGHTS RESERVED. INTERNATIONAL COPYRIGHT SECURED.

Introduction

This hit by The Crickets—led of course by Buddy Holly—was also the first song to be recorded by The Quarrymen, John Lennon's pre-Beatles skiffle combo.

Intro Riff

The original version of this song uses a capo (fret 5)—but if you play it like that you'd need to know barre chord shapes that we're not going to cover at this stage. So, this arrangement allows you to play along with the record using the chords you know.

There's an intro riff to this song which we've arranged here so you can play it without the capo; it's not exactly like the original but it'll sound cool for now!

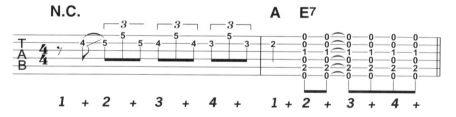

Strumming

Use a regular shuffle strumming pattern and later on, try the 12-Bar Blues Shuffle.

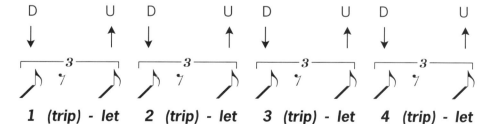

STAGE 6 BC-161—BC-169

 ## Introduction

This stage introduces the F chord, which is the chord most people really struggle with. I sure did, and used to avoid any songs that had F… but you can't avoid it forever, so it's best to just confront it and get in there and try out some of these songs. It just takes practice! I know it can feel impossible, and that you will never get it, but it is easier than it first feels. It takes a bit of time to build up the strength to hold it right and then get the changes to and from it as well. Make sure you keep up the One-Minute Changes (BC-162).

We also introduce a strumming pattern that uses a tie, which is probably the most commonly-used strumming pattern of all time (and a really cool sounding one!). It sounds more 'natural' than the other ones we have looked at so far. It can take a bit of time to get used to, but keep your hand moving consistently, stick at it, do it slowly—correctly—and it will become instinctive in no time!

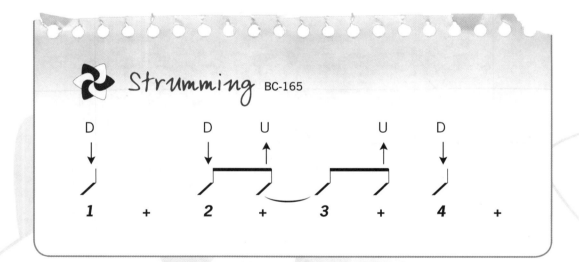

Stage 6 Chords

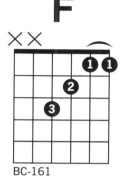
F
BC-161

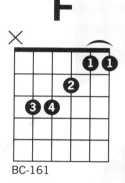
F
BC-161

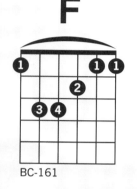
F
BC-161

Stage 6: Your notes

Please Forgive Me
Words & Music by David Gray

Intro

‖: C | Em | Am | G :‖

Verse 1

```
C          Em        Am          G
Please for - give me if I act a little strange
C       Em          Am    G
For I know not what I do.
C           Em             Am            G
Feels like lightning running through my veins
F       F            C   G
Every - time I look at you
F       F
Every - time I look at you.
```

| C | Em | Am | G |

(you.)

Verse 2

Help me out here, all my words are falling short
And there's so much I want to say.
Want to tell you just how good it feels
When you look at me that way
When you look at me that way.

‖: C | Em | Am | G :‖

(way.)

Verse 3

Throw a stone and watch the ripples flow
Moving out across the bay.
Like a stone I fall into your eyes
Deep into that mystery
Deep into some mystery.

| C | Em | Am | G |

Verse 4

I got half a mind to scream out loud
I got half a mind to die
So I won't ever have to lose you girl
Won't ever have to say goodbye
I won't ever have to lie
Won't ever have to say goodbye.

‖: C | Em | Am | G :‖ *Play x3*

                Woh woh woh I

| F | F | C | G |
| F | F | | |

Verse 5   As Verse 1

© COPYRIGHT 1998 CHRYSALIS MUSIC LIMITED.
ALL RIGHTS RESERVED. INTERNATIONAL COPYRIGHT SECURED.

Introduction

This song was the third single from David Gray's mega-selling *White Ladder* album, released in 1999.

 ## Melodic parts

You can add a little melodic element to the rhythm part in this song by starting your up-strums from the second string. Most us will hear the highest note as the melody, so playing from the second string will make the C note the melody on the first chord. The melody for the second chord (Em) goes from C to B, so add in the note C (second string, 1st fret) with your 1st finger to your Em chord (using fingers 2 and 3 for the Em) for the first up-strum, then lift it off for the second. The third chord is Am, which already has the note C, which we play for both up-strums. The last chord in the sequence is G, so we use a special fingering that will allow us to use our first finger to play the note C then B on the up-strums as before. This might be a stretch, but will come with a little practice! See the chord boxes below:

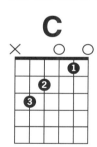   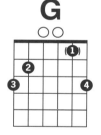

Strumming

This song sounds best played with the syncopated rhythm shown below. You can add in some other strums to 'fill it out' a bit if you like, but getting this pattern right will make it sound really cool, especially if you get the melodic element (above) in there too.

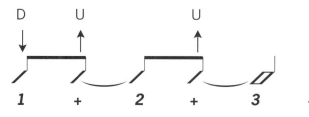

I'm A Believer
Words & Music by Neil Diamond

Intro

```
            riff
| G7   C  | (D7)    | (D7)    ||
```

Verse 1

G   D   G   G
I thought love was only true in fairy tales,
                   D   G   G
Meant for someone else but not for me.
C   G   C
Love was out to get me (da da da da da),
             G   C
That's the way it seems (da da da da da),
             G   D7   D7
Disappointment haunted all my dreams.

Chorus 1

```
                    | G  C | G   C |  G   C |
Then I saw her face,       now I'm a be - liever.
| G C | G   C G  C |   G   C |
   Not a trace    of doubt in my mind,
| G C | G   C |    G
   I'm in love, oh, I'm a be - liever,
                 riff
       F        (D7)   (D7)
I couldn't leave her if I tried.
```

Verse 2

I thought love was more or less a given thing,
It seems the more I gave the less I got.
What's the use in trying (da da da da da),
All you get is pain (da da da da da),
When I needed sunshine I got rain.

Chorus 2

As Chorus 1

Solo

```
||: G7   | D7   | G7   | G7   :||
```

Verse 3

Love was out to get me, that's the way it seems,
Disappointment haunted all my dreams.

Chorus 3

As Chorus 1

Outro

Repeat chorus *ad lib.*

© COPYRIGHT 1966 STONEBRIDGE MUSIC INCORPORATED/COLGEMS-EMI MUSIC INCORPORATED.
SCREEN GEMS-EMI MUSIC PUBLISHING LIMITED/SONY/ATV MUSIC PUBLISHING.
ALL RIGHTS RESERVED. INTERNATIONAL COPYRIGHT SECURED.

Introduction

Younger guitarists may associate this song with Eddie Murphy in the movie *Shrek*, but the definitive recording of this Neil Diamond song is by the Monkees, who produced a hit so huge that by the end of 1966, it had sold over 10 million copies.

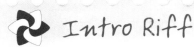 ### Intro Riff

This song will give you a chance to use some of your 7th chords and to get in some F chord action too, albeit only briefly! Watch out for the held chords at the end of the chorus, starting on the word 'love'. Play them once, and let each chord ring out until you reach the D7 chord, where you could try the catchy little riff, which I've written out for you below. The solo also has a great riff, so if you come back to this tune as a more advanced player you'll want to work it out—it's based on the G minor pentatonic scale.

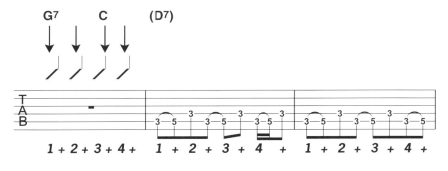

Strumming

If you listen to the Monkees recording, you'll hear the guitar playing very heavy accents on beats 2 and 4, giving the song a solid backbeat. To emphasize these accents you'll need to play the down-strums on beats 2 and 4 a little louder, and make the other strums a little quieter.

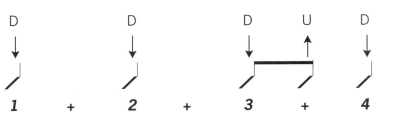

Dakota

Words & Music by Kelly Jones

Capo Fret 4

Intro

‖: C | C | Am | Am | Fmaj7 | Fmaj7 | C | C :‖

Verse 1

```
   C  C                    Am
   Thinking back, thinking of you,
   Am           Fmaj7 Fmaj7             C  C
   Summertime, think it was June,   yeah I think it was June.
   C  C                    Am
   Laying back, head on the grass,
   Am           Fmaj7 Fmaj7                  C  |C G|
   Chewing gum, having some laughs,   yeah having some laughs.
```

Chorus 1

```
   F        F            F
   You made me feel like the one,
            F       C  C   C  |C G|
   You made me feel like the one,  the one.
```

Verse 2

Drinking back, drinking for two, drinking with you, when drinking was new.
Sleeping in the back of my car, we never went far, didn't need to go far.

Chorus 2

As Chorus 1 *(Play x2)*

Bridge 1

```
   C    C      G  G    F  F  F
   I don't know where we are going now,
   C    C      G  G    F  F  F
   I don't know where we are going now.
```

Verse 3

Wake up call, coffee and juice, remembering you,
What happened to you?
I wonder if we'll meet again?
Talk about life since then, talk about why did it end.

Chorus 3 As Chorus 2
Bridge 2 As Bridge 1

Outro

So take a look at me now... *(Repeat until end)*

‖: C | C | G | G | F | F | F | F :‖

‖: C | C | Am | Am | F | F | F | F :‖ C

© COPYRIGHT 2005 STEREOPHONICS MUSIC LIMITED.
UNIVERSAL MUSIC PUBLISHING LIMITED.
ALL RIGHTS RESERVED. INTERNATIONAL COPYRIGHT SECURED.

Introduction

Stereophonics' first UK No. 1 single also paved the way for their US breakthrough in 2005, helped by a music video filmed in—you guessed it—Dakota.

Capo

This is a great party tune, and Kelly plays it like this—with a capo on the 4th fret—for live acoustic versions. You might like to work out the electric guitar melody line in the chorus if you are playing it with another guitar player.

Strumming

This song works best if you strum eight constant down-strokes per bar. At first it can be tricky to play fast down-strokes for the whole song, but with a little practice, it'll get much easier. I must admit, I often cheat and switch to down/up-strumming (strumming up on the 'ands') in the chorus to give myself a break! Remember to make the pattern quieter during the verses and louder in the choruses as this will give it some dynamic variation and keep it interesting for your audience.

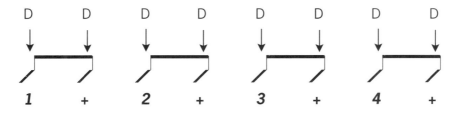

No Woman, No Cry
Words & Music by Vincent Ford

Capo Fret 1

Chorus 1
```
||: C     G      |Am    F |C     F     |C     G  :||
   No woman, no  cry,     no woman, no cry.
```

Verse 1
```
   |C        G      |Am                F    |
    Say, say, said  I remember when we used to sit
   C         G      |Am             F        |
    In the government yard in Trenchtown,
   C         G      |Am             F        |
    Oba-observing the hypocrites
   |C         G            |Am              F  |
    As they  would mingle with the good people we meet.
   C           G          |Am              F    |
    Good friends we have had, oh good friends we've lost
   C  G       |Am    F |
    Along the way.
   C         G           |Am             F       |
    In this bright future you can't forget your past,
   C           G      |Am   F  |
    So dry your tears, I say, and
```

Chorus 2
No woman, no cry, no woman, no cry,
Here little darlin', don't shed no tears, No woman, no cry.

Verse 2
Said, said, said I remember when we used to sit
In the government yard in Trenchtown,
And then Georgie would make the fire light
As it was log wood burnin' through the night.
Then we would cook corn meal porridge
Of which I'll share with you.
My feet is my only carriage
So I've got to push on through.

Bridge
```
||: |C                G       |
       Ev'rything's gonna be alright,
    |Am              F  G     |
       Ev'rything's gonna be alright.  :||  Play x4
```

Chorus 3   As Chorus 2

Solo
```
||: C  G  |Am  F  |C  F  |C  G  :||  Play x4
```

Verse 3   As Verse 2

Chorus 4   As Chorus 2 (x2)

© COPYRIGHT 1974 FIFTY-SIX HOPE ROAD MUSIC LIMITED/ODNIL MUSIC LIMITED.
BLUE MOUNTAIN MUSIC LIMITED.
ALL RIGHTS RESERVED. INTERNATIONAL COPYRIGHT SECURED.

Introduction

Perhaps Bob Marley's best-known song, this anthem of struggle and freedom first appeared on the Wailers' 1974 album *Natty Dread*.

Reggae feel

Reggae music has a very specific feel to it, and to get in the right groove it's very important that you actually listen to some. So look up some Bob Marley albums (try the compilation *Legend* for starters) and try to absorb the feel, play along and try to 'lock in'. You should notice when you get it right, it feels right. You won't be wondering if it's right —you will know it! Locking into a groove takes practice like everything else, but you should find as you get used to it that it happens sooner and better. The trick (if there is one) is to make sure you focus on the drums!

Once you've finished the course, come back and change each G chord to G/B—that's what is played on the original version.

Playing the off beats

Reggae rhythm is all about the up-strums—the off-beats—and it's part of what defines the style. However, this kind of rhythm works best in conjunction with the rest of the band, and so it can sound a little strange if you are playing on your own. So this pattern that I'm going to show you here is a great one to work on. All I have added is a down-strum on beats 1 and 3. Just play these softly, emphasizing the thick strings (with the ands mostly on the thin strings) and you will feel the groove shift a bit. I think playing this way sounds great when you are playing on your own.

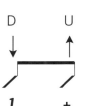

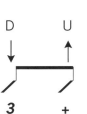

Can't Help Falling In Love

Words & Music by George David Weiss, Hugo Peretti & Luigi Creatore

Capo Fret **2**

Intro | C | G | C | C |

Verse 1
C   Em   Am
Wise men say
Am   F   C   G7   G7
Only fools rush in
F   G   Am
But I can't help
F   C   G7   C   C
Falling in love with you.

Verse 2
Shall I stay,
Would it be a sin,
If I can't help falling in love with you?

Bridge 1
Em   B7
Like a river flows
Em   B7
Surely to the sea,
Em   B7
Darling so it goes:
Em   A7   Dm   G7
Some things are meant to be.

Verse 3
Take my hand,
Take my whole life too,
For I can't help falling in love with you.

Bridge 2 As Bridge 1

Verse 4
Take my hand,
Take my whole life too,
For I can't help falling in love with you,
For I can't help falling in love with you.

© COPYRIGHT 1961 GLADYS MUSIC.
ALL RIGHTS RESERVED. INTERNATIONAL COPYRIGHT SECURED.

Introduction

UB40 had a big hit with their reggae version of this song in 1993, but these chords are for the original version by Elvis Presley.

 ## Playing ballads

Playing a slow ballad is all about sensitivity. Use a thin pick (or use a medium pick and hold it lightly) and think about stroking the strings, caress them, be gentle. Try and show some love through the instrument! I know that sounds really corny, but that is the way to think about it, and it will make all the difference to the listener!

Keep it Simple!

This one can be played many ways. I like to play it fingerstyle myself, but one of the most amazing versions I ever heard was by a girl in Nashville who just played down-strums. Really simple. It was amazing, (though it didn't hurt that she had the voice of an angel!)… it's all about the feeling. So try it with all down-strums as shown, with the emphasis on beats 1 and 4. Playing more complex stuff won't add much to a wonderful song like this. Can you put the feel into it to make it beautiful?

Once you can play some finger-picking you might like to try it with this song. Pick six notes for each chord.

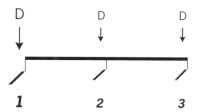 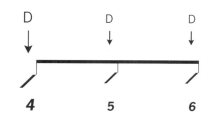

Pink Bullets

Words & Music by James Mercer

Capo Fret 3

Intro $\|:$ Em $\quad$ |D A $:\|$ *Play x4*

Verse 1

Em |D   A |Em |D   A |
I was just bony hands as cold as a winter pole
Em |D   A |Em |D   A |
You held a warm stone out new flowing blood to hold
Em |D   A |Em |D   A |
Oh what a con - trast you were   to the brutes in the halls
Em |D   A |Em |D   A |
My timid young fingers held a decent animal

Chorus 1

G   D
Over the ram - parts you tossed
G   D
The scent of your skin and some foreign flowers
G   D   F
Tied to a brick sweet as a song
                       C   D   D
The years have been short but the days were long

Verse 2

Cool of a temperate breeze from dark skies to wet grass
We fell in a field it seems now a thousand summers passed
When our kite lines first crossed we tied them into knots
And to finally fly apart we had to cut them off

Chorus 2

Since then it's been a book you read in reverse
So you understand less as the pages turn
Or a movie so crass and awkwardly cast
          C   G   G
That even I could be the star

Bridge

C D   F   G
   I don't look back much as a rule
C D   F   G
   And all this way before murder is cool
C   D   G   C
But your memory is here and I'd like you to stay
C   D   D
   A warm light   on a winter's day

Chorus 3

Over the ramparts you tossed
The scent of your skin and some foreign flowers
Tied to a brick sweet as a song
The years have seemed short but the days go slowly by
To loose kites falling from the sky
Drawn to the ground and an end to flight

© COPYRIGHT 2003 LETTUCE FLAVORED MUSIC, USA.
EMI MUSIC PUBLISHING LIMITED.
ALL RIGHTS RESERVED. INTERNATIONAL COPYRIGHT SECURED.

Introduction

This song by The Shins featured on their sophomore album *Chutes Too Narrow* in 2003.

Frilly bits!

On the original recording you can hear the acoustic guitar do a little flurry of notes on the A chord. It's a very fast hammer-on, flick-off combination with the little finger going down on the second string, 3rd fret (the note D) and then flicking off the note on the 2nd fret of the second string to the open. The rhythm is a little awkward too, and will most likely take a bit of practice to get it right, but it does sound super-cool once you've got it.

Bass Note Strum

This one is using the bass note followed by a down- and up-strum shown in lesson BC-175. It's a great example of that strum pattern. Start off by getting the chords and changes solid and by the time you are confident with that, you'll probably be learning this cool strumming in Stage 7 and be able to use it in this song right away. Remember that you must know the bass root note for each chord as that is the one you will play on beats 1 and 3.

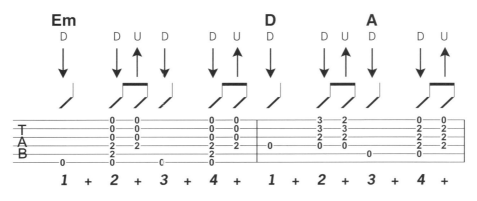

The Thrill Is Gone
Words & Music by Roy Hawkins & Rick Darnell

Capo Fret 2

Intro

| drums |

| Am | Am | Am | Am |

| Dm | Dm | Am | Am |

| Fmaj7 | E7 | Am | Am |

Verse 1

    Am   Am   Am   Am
The thrill is gone,   the thrill is gone away.
    Dm   Dm   Am   Am
The thrill is gone baby,   the thrill is gone a - way.
Fmaj7   E7   Am   Am
You know you done me wrong,   baby, and you'll be sorry someday.

Verse 2

The thrill is gone, it's gone away from me.
The thrill is gone baby, the thrill is gone away from me.
Although, I'll still live on, but so lonely I'll be.

Solo 1   As Verse chords

Verse 3

The thrill is gone, it's gone away for good.
Oh, the thrill is gone baby, it's gone away for good.
Someday I know I'll be holding on, baby,
Just like I know a good man should.

Verse 4

You know I'm free, free now baby, I'm free from your spell.
Oh, I'm free, free, free now, I'm free from your spell.
And now that it's all over, all I can do is wish you well.

Solo 2   As Verse chords

Outro

|: Am | Am :| *Repeat to fade*

© COPYRIGHT 1951 CAREERS-BMG MUSIC PUBLISHING INCORPORATED, USA.
UNIVERSAL MUSIC PUBLISHING MGB LIMITED.
(A DIVISION OF UNIVERSAL MUSIC PUBLISHING GROUP).
ALL RIGHTS RESERVED. INTERNATIONAL COPYRIGHT SECURED.

Introduction

One of the greatest B.B. King songs. Check out the original for B.B.'s awesome solo and also the cool rhythm parts played by Hugh McCracken.

The Backbeat

The backbeat is the accent created by the snare drum and it is very important to be aware of it. Whenever you play you should make sure your down-strums on beats 2 and 4 synchronize exactly with the drum hit on those beats. Because the snare drum is so clearly heard it sounds great if you emphasize those two beats in your rhythm patterns, especially if you are playing by yourself (without accompaniment).
Be sure to realize that if you start too loudly you won't be able to make the accent, so start quietly!

Strumming

There are many strum patterns that would work well with this song, and by using accents you will be able to get a great feel. If you get the accent right it should sound cool—this pattern works well—but be sure to experiment with others too. In a band situation you might like to try playing only on beats 2 and 4!

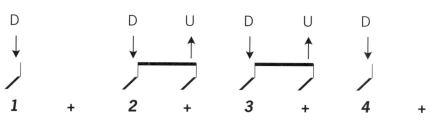

Mr. Jones

Words & Music by Adam Duritz, David Bryson, Matthew Malley, Steve Bowman & Charles Gillingham

Verse 1

    Am   F   Dm   G
I was down at the New Amsterdam   staring at this yellow-haired girl,
   Am   F   G   G
Mr. Jones strikes up a conver - sation with a black-haired flamenco dancer.
       Am   F   Dm   G
You know she dances while his father plays gui - tar, she's suddenly beautiful.
       Am   F   G   G
And we all want something beautiful,   man, I wish I was beautiful.

Verse 2

So come dance this silence down through the morning,
Sha la la la la la la la, yeah. Uh huh, yeah.
Cut up, Maria! Show me some of them Spanish dances,
And pass me a bottle, Mr. Jones.
Believe in me, help me believe in anything,
'Cause I wanna be someone who believes, yeah.

Chorus 1

  C   F   G   G
   Mr. Jones and me   tell each other fairy tales
      C   F
And we stare at the beautiful women.
  G   G   C
"She's looking at you. Ah no, no, she's looking at me."
       F   G   G
Smiling in the bright lights,   coming through in stereo.
        C   F   G   G
When everybody loves   you,   you can never be lonely.

Verse 3

Well I'm gonna paint my picture,
Paint myself in blue and red and black and grey,
All of the beautiful colours are very, very meaningful.
Yeah well you know grey is my favourite colour, I felt so symbolic, yesterday,
If I knew Picasso, I would buy myself a grey guitar and play.

Chorus 2

Mr. Jones and me look into the future,
Yeah, we stare at the beautiful women,
"She's looking at you. I don't think so. She's looking at me."
Standing in the spotlight, I bought myself a grey guitar.
When everybody loves me, I will never be lonely.

Middle

Am   Am   Fmaj7 Fmaj7   Am   Am   G   G
 I will never be lonely,   said I'm never gonna be, lonely.
Am   Am Fmaj7   Fmaj7
 I wanna be a lion,   and everybody wants to pass as cats,
Am   Am   G   G
We all want to be big, big stars, yeah but we got different reasons for that.
Am   Am   Fmaj7   Fmaj7
 Believe in me, because I don't believe in anything
Am   Am   G   G
And I, I wanna be someone to believe, to believe, to believe, yeah.

© COPYRIGHT 1993 EMI BLACKWOOD MUSIC INCORPORATED/JONES FALLS MUSIC, USA.
EMI MUSIC PUBLISHING LIMITED.
ALL RIGHTS RESERVED. INTERNATIONAL COPYRIGHT SECURED.

Chorus 3 Mr. Jones and me stumbling through the barrio
Yeah, we stare at the beautiful women,
"She's perfect for you, man, there's got to be somebody for me."
I want to be Bob Dylan,
Mr. Jones wishes he was someone just a little more funky
And then everybody loves you, oh son,
That's just about as funky as you can be.

Chorus 4 Mr. Jones and me staring at the video,
When I look at the television I want to see me
Staring right back at me.
We all want to be big stars,
But we don't know why and we don't know how
But when everybody loves me
I wanna be just about as happy as I can be.
Mr. Jones and me: we're gonna be big stars.

Introduction

Counting Crows' debut single and their biggest hit. The chords are straightforward but it might take some practice to remember all those words…

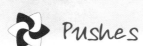

Pushes

Sometimes chord changes do not always fall on the beat, and commonly the chords change on the 'and', or up-strum, before beat 1. This is called a 'push' because it pushes the chord change half a beat early. Just by listening closely to the track a number of times you might find that you start to do it naturally, I was playing pushes for at least ten years before I knew they had a name and did it consciously!

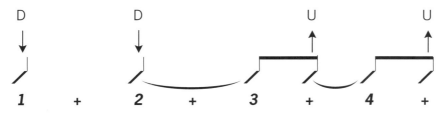

The Drugs Don't Work
Words & Music by Richard Ashcroft

Intro

|C |C |Am |Am |

|Em |F   G |C   G |C ||

Verse 1

          C   C   Am
All this talk of getting old,   it's getting me down my love.
 Am   Em |F   G |C   G|C
  Like a cat in a bag, waiting to drown, this time I'm coming down.

Verse 2

          C   C   Am
And I hope you're thinking of me,   as you lay down on your side.
 Am   Em |F
  Now the drugs don't work, they just make you worse
  G |C   G|
But I know I'll see your face again.
    C   Em |F
  Now the drugs don't work, they just make you worse
  G |C   G|C
But I know I'll see your face again.

Verse 3

        C   C   Am   Am
But I know I'm on a losing streak, as I pass down my old street.
               Em |F   G |C   G|
And if you want a show, just let me know and I'll sing in your ear again.
    C   Em |F
  Now the drugs don't work, they just make you worse
  G |C   G|C
But I know I'll see your face again,   'cause baby,

Bridge 1

 F   Em   Am   G
Ooh,   if heaven calls, I'm coming too.
               F   Em   Am   G
Just like you say,   you'll leave my life, I'm better off dead.

Verse 4

All this talk of getting old, it's getting me down my love.
Like a cat in a bag waiting to drown, this time I'm coming down
Now the drugs don't work, they just make you worse
But I know I'll see your face again, 'cause baby.

Bridge 2

As Bridge 1
               Em |F   G |C   G|
And if you want a show, just let me know and I'll sing in your ear again.
    C   Em |F
  Now the drugs don't work, they just make you worse
  G |C   G|
But I know I'll see your face again.
||:C   G |C   G :||
  Yeah I know I'll see your face again.   *(Repeat ad lib. to end)*

© COPYRIGHT 1997 EMI VIRGIN MUSIC LIMITED.
ALL RIGHTS RESERVED. INTERNATIONAL COPYRIGHT SECURED.

justinguitar

Introduction

After years of break-ups and turmoil, The Verve returned in 1997 with this moving ballad. It's a tale of love and loss, and a great closer to any set. Watch out for the tuning—the recording is slightly flatter than standard pitch.

Playing with a Friend

This is a wonderful song to play and sing along to. For me, it works best with two guitar players, one strumming on an acoustic and the other player on either acoustic or clean electric, picking out notes from the chords. To play this second part, follow the same chords, but instead of strumming, just pick a few notes per bar and let them ring out—you can hear this clearly on the original recording and it sounds really cool. So grab a buddy who plays and have a go at it!

Strumming

The strumming patterns in this song vary quite a lot, so if you want to get the patterns down perfectly, listen to the recording a few times and try to feel it out. What I have below is a typical pattern. It uses sixteenth-note strumming—which we don't cover in the beginner's course—so I have written it as two bars of eighth-notes, but remember that you'll have to play the whole two bars each time a chord is written. If you feel the pattern below is a bit too advanced, you can easily play any of the simpler patterns we've used previously.

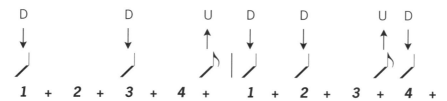

House Of The Rising Sun
Traditional

Intro |Am |C |D |F |Am |E |Am |E |

Verse 1
     Am C   **D**   **F**
There is a house in New Orleans
     Am   **C**   **E**   **E**
They call the Rising Sun
       Am   **C**   **D**   **F**
And it's been the ruin of many a poor boy
     Am   **E**
And God I know, I'm (one.)

|Am |C |D |F |Am |E |Am |E |
one.

Verse 2
My mother was a tailor,
She sewed my new blue jeans.
My father was a gambling man
Down in New Orleans.

Verse 3
Now the only thing a gambler needs
Is a suitcase and a trunk,
And the only time he's satisfied
Is when he's all a-drunk.

Verse 4
Oh mother, tell your children
Not to do what I have done.
Spend your lives in sin and misery
In the house of the Rising Sun.

Verse 5
Well I've got one foot on the platform,
The other foot on the train.
I'm going back to New Orleans
To wear that ball and chain.

Verse 6 As Verse 1

Coda |Am |C |D |F |Am |E |

‖: Am | Dm | Am | Dm :‖ Am | Dm | Am |

Introduction

This song was a big hit for The Animals in 1964, but has much older folk music origins. Other key recordings include those by Leadbelly, Joan Baez and Bob Dylan.

 ## A Feel of Three

This song has a rolling feel with two beats in each bar and each beat divided into three. In proper music terms this is called 6/8 time, as we saw for 'This Year's Love' (page 68) and 'Can't Help Falling In Love' (page 126). What this means is that you could either play each chord twice, slowly, each time it's written, or play each chord with six faster strums in each bar. I would recommend using all down-strums though to make sure you get a good groove, regardless of whether you are doing two or six strums in the bar.

Fingerstyle pattern

This song is also very good fun to play using fingerstyle using the 6/8 pattern T 1 2 3 2 1, where T is the Thumb and plays the bass note and the 1st, 2nd and 3rd fingers play the third, second and first strings respectively. Playing fingerstyle really helps you make sure that your chord grips are good, because as you play the notes one at a time, there is no hiding a dead note! There is a full lesson on fingerstyle in Stage 9 of the beginners course, lesson BC-193.

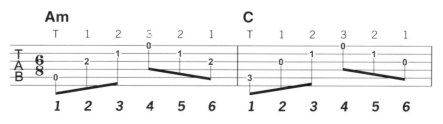

STAGE 7 BC-171—BC-179

 ## Introduction

In this stage we have some really interesting chord types—power chords (BC-172)—which are a great introduction to barre chords (which are covered in the Intermediate Method) and are used in many rock and pop songs. They are pretty easy to play and will help you remember the notes on the thickest string (see opposite). We look at chords with a sixth string root in Stage 7 and with a fifth string root in Stage 8 (Page 160), but when playing songs you can mix up the fifth and sixth string roots as you like.

Power chords are very useful: sometimes you will find a song where you know all the chords except one or two and it's kind of annoying. For example, a song might look easy, except that you see Bm in the chord progression, which you haven't learnt yet. Grrrr! But there is a trick: any chord can be substituted for a power chord, because power chords are neither major or minor. So rather than stress about not playing the Bm, just play a B power chord (B5) instead, and then you can play the tune, and later on, when you've learnt the Bm barre chord you can come back and add that chord in.

We also learn about using suspended (sus) chords (BC-173), which will really add interest to your rhythm playing once you get them down. It's important to practise using them in context, but also as an exercise on their own, so get in there with your One-Minute Changes (BC-174) for these and then work them into your songs. You can of course use them in the songs shown in this stage, but you can also add them into other songs too, so a great exercise would be to go back through the songs you have mastered so far and try to work some in. Just try to hear where they might sound. Don't be scared to make a mistake: you will soon develop a feel for when they will work and when they won't!

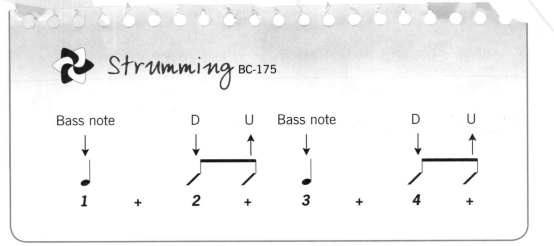

Stage 7 Chords

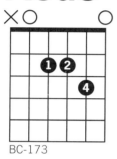
Asus⁴
BC-173

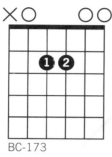
Asus²
BC-173

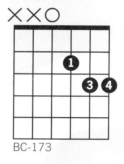
Dsus⁴
BC-173

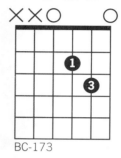
Dsus²
BC-173

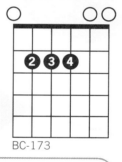
Esus⁴
BC-173

Power Chords BC-172

The diagram on the left shows the guitar neck and the names of the natural notes on the thickest (E) string. You should memorise this so that you can find any power chord shape with its root on this string. For instance, G5 can be found at the 3rd fret.

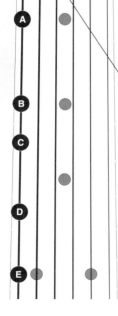

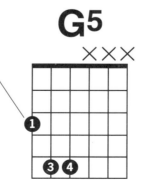
G5

Summer Of '69
Words & Music by Bryan Adams & Jim Vallance

Intro
| D⁵ | D⁵ |

Verse 1
D⁵   D⁵   A⁵   A⁵
I got my first real six-string,   bought it at the five-and-dime.
D⁵   D⁵   A⁵   A⁵
Played it 'til my fingers bled,   it was the summer of sixty-nine.

Verse 2
Me and some guys from school had a band and we tried real hard.
Jimmy quit and Jody got married, I should've known we'd never get far.

Chorus 1
B⁵   A
Oh, when I look back now,
D   G
That summer seemed to last forever,
B⁵   A
And if I had the choice
D   G
Yeah, I'd always wanna be there.
B⁵   A   D   D   A   A
Those were the best days of my life.   **(with riff)**

Verse 3
Ain't no use in complainin' when you got a job to do.
Spent my evenings down at the drive-in, and that's when I met you, yeah!

Chorus 2
Standin' on your Mama's porch,
You told me that you'd wait forever.
Oh, and when you held my hand
I knew that it was now or never.
Those were the best days of my life, oh yeah
Back in the summer of sixty-nine.

Bridge
F⁵   B♭⁵   C⁵
Man, we were killin' time, we were young and restless,
B♭⁵
We needed to unwind.
F⁵   B♭⁵   C⁵   C⁵
I guess nothin' can last forever, forever, no.

Link
| D | D | A | A | D | D | A | A |
(with riff)

Verse 4
And now the times are changin', look at everything that's come and gone.
Sometimes when I play that old six-string
I think about you, wonder what went wrong.

Chorus 3
As Chorus 2 (*Repeat riff to fade*)

© COPYRIGHT 1984 ALMO MUSIC CORPORATION/ADAMS COMMUNICATIONS
INCORPORATED/TESTATYME MUSIC/IRVING MUSIC CORPORATION, USA.
RONDOR MUSIC (LONDON) LIMITED.
ALL RIGHTS IN GERMANY ADMINISTERED BY RONDOR MUSIKVERLAG GMBH.
ALL RIGHTS RESERVED. INTERNATIONAL COPYRIGHT SECURED.

justinguitar

🌀 Introduction
Be sure to learn how to play this if you want to gig in a pub…

🌀 Sus Chords Riff

This riff (played on a keyboard on the recording) uses the D and A suspended chords you have learnt in this stage (BC-173). You can play it with your pick or as fingerstyle if you prefer. It's as simple as playing your regular D and A chords, but lifting a finger off or adding your little finger for a few notes.

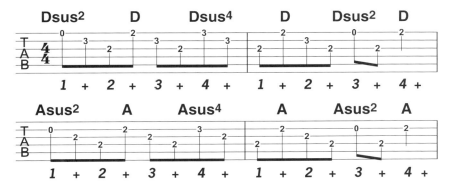

🌀 Strumming

The strumming in this song is generally played using all down-strums, with the rhythmic interest developed using accents. This kind of strumming is very clearly heard in the intro, where the accents are on beats 1 and the 'and' after 2, but a similar technique is used for the rest of the song too.

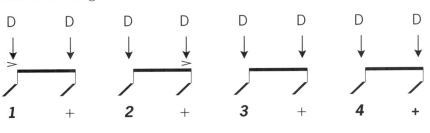

141

Wanted Dead Or Alive

Words & Music by Richie Sambora & Jon Bon Jovi

Intro

‖: Dm (with riff) | Dm | Dm | Dm :‖

Verse 1

    D |C   G |
It's all the same, only the name will change,
C   G |F   D |
Every day it seems we're wasting away.
D |C   G
Another place where the faces are so cold,
 |C   G |F   D
I'd drive all night just to get back home.

Chorus 1

 |C   G |F   D |
I'm a cowboy,   on a steel horse I ride,
 |C   G |F   D |
I'm wanted   dead or a - live,
 |C   G |F   D | Dm (with riff)
I'm wanted   dead or a - live.

Verse 2

Sometimes I sleep, sometimes it's not for days,
The people I meet they just go their separate ways.
Sometimes you tell the day by the bottle that you drink,
Sometimes when you're alone all you do is think.

Chorus 2

As Chorus 1

Instrumental

Guitar solo as verse

Chorus 3

As Chorus 2

Verse 3

And I walk these streets, a loaded six-string on my back,
I play for keeps 'cause I might not make it back.
I've been everywhere and still I'm standing tall,
I've seen a million faces and I've rocked them all.

Chorus 4

'Cause I'm a cowboy, on a steel horse I ride,
I'm wanted dead or alive.
And I'm a cowboy, I got the night on my side,
And I'm wanted dead or alive.
And I ride (and I ride),
Dead or alive,
I still jive (I still jive),
Dead or alive…

Outro

| Dm | Dm | Dm | Dm D |

© COPYRIGHT 1986 BON JOVI PUBLISHING/POLYGRAM INTERNATIONAL MUSIC PUBLISHING INCORPORATED, USA.
SONY/ATV MUSIC PUBLISHING (50%)/UNIVERSAL MUSIC PUBLISHING LIMITED (50%).
ALL RIGHTS RESERVED. INTERNATIONAL COPYRIGHT SECURED.

Introduction

Bon Jovi's Western-themed classic from their *Slippery When Wet* album (1986).

Intro Riff

This intro riff is a very memorable part of the song and it is not very hard to play. Make sure you use your 2nd finger for all the notes on the third string. Use your 1st finger if the note on the thinnest string is one lower than the note on the third string, and use your 3rd finger when the note on the thinnest string is in the same fret as the note on the third string.

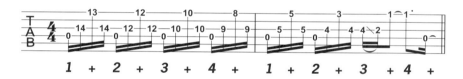

Strumming Patterns

The strumming on the original recorded version is pretty complex for beginners and uses sixteenth-note strumming, but it's such a fun song to play, I would suggest you learn it using the simplified pattern shown below and revisit it after you are feeling confident with your sixteenth-note strumming patterns.

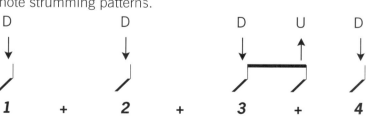

Lucky Man
Words & Music by Richard Ashcroft

Verse 1

|G   D |
Happiness more or less,
Asus⁴
It's just a change in me something in my levity
|G   D |Asus⁴
Ooh my,   my.
|G   D |
Happiness coming and going,
Asus⁴
I watch you look at me watch my fever grow I know
|G   D |Asus⁴
Just where I am.

Chorus 1

        Em
Well, how many corners do I have to turn
G
How many times do I have to learn
D   **Asus⁴**
All the love I have is in my mind.
       |G   D |Asus⁴
But I'm a lucky man
       |G   D |Asus⁴
With fire in my hands.

Verse 2

Happiness something in my own place,
I'm stood here naked smiling I feel no disgrace
With who I am
Happiness coming and going,
I watch you look at me watch my fever growing,
I know just who I am.

Chorus 2   As Chorus 1

Bridge

      |G   D |Asus⁴
Ooh_____, no, no, no, no, no, no, no, no,
      |G   D | Asus⁴
Gotta love that never dies

Chorus 3   As Chorus 1

© COPYRIGHT 1997 EMI VIRGIN MUSIC LIMITED.
ALL RIGHTS RESERVED. INTERNATIONAL COPYRIGHT SECURED.

Introduction

The Verve's 1997 album *Urban Hymns* spawned three Top Ten singles, of which this was the third.

 Adding Sus Chords

This is a really great tune to use your sus chords on the A (so, Asus4 and Asus2) and D (Dsus4 and Dsus2). Listen to the original recording and you will hear them clearly. You can choose to put them in the same places as the record or you can have fun experimenting.

Strumming

This one uses strumming in sixteenth-notes, but rather than worry about all that, just listen and keep your hand moving evenly and consistently in down-strokes along with the track and then start experimenting with the placement of accents, adding up-strums in between them. It's kind of tricky to get all the patterns in the same exact order as the recording, so be cool with getting close and experimenting yourself.

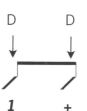 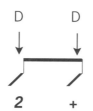 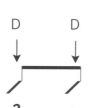 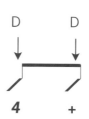

California Dreamin'
Music by John Phillips & Michelle Gilliam

Capo Fret **4**

Intro

| Asus²   Asus⁴   Am | Asus²   Asus⁴   Am |

| Asus²   Asus⁴   Am | E⁷sus⁴ |

Verse 1

```
        |Am    G F    G     |E7sus4 | E7
All the leaves are brown,   and the sky is grey,
F       |C   E7|Am    F     |E7sus4 | E7
I've been for a walk,    on a winter's day.
        |Am   G|F    G      |E7sus4 | E7
I'd be safe and warm,   If I was in L.A.
```

Chorus 1

```
        |Am   G|F    G      |E7sus4 | E7sus4 |
California dreamin'     on such a winter's day. ___
```

Verse 2

Stopped into a church, I passed along the way,
Well, I got down on my knees, and I pretend to pray.
You know the preacher like the cold, he knows I'm gonna stay.

Chorus 2   As Chorus 1

Flute solo

| Am | Am | Am | Am   F |

| C   E⁷ | Am   F | E⁷sus⁴ | E⁷ |

‖: Am   G | F   G | E⁷sus⁴ | E⁷   :‖

Verse 3

All the leaves are brown, and the sky is grey,
I've been for a walk on a winter's day.
If I didn't tell her, I could leave today.

Outro

```
        |Am   G |
California dreamin'
F   G   |Am    G |
 On such a winter's day,
F   G   |Am    G |
 On such a winter's day,
F   G   |Fmaj7 Am |
 On such a winter's day. ___
```

© COPYRIGHT 1965 WINGUS MUSIC PUBLISHING INCORPORATED.
UNIVERSAL/MCA MUSIC LIMITED.
ALL RIGHTS RESERVED. INTERNATIONAL COPYRIGHT SECURED.

Introduction

A '60s song with timeless appeal, this was first a hit for The Mamas and The Papas in 1965.

E7sus4

This song has a very cool chord in it that is a little unusual, but easy to play—E7sus4. The chord is usually followed by E7, so start with that (using your 1st and 2nd fingers) and then put your 3rd finger down in the 2nd fret of the third string, in front of your 1st finger. Even though you don't really need to hold your 1st finger down, it's better to leave it so it's ready when you lift off your 3rd finger for the E7. A new one for your chord book!

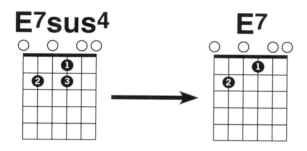

Strumming

This two-bar pattern is a little tricky, but slow practice will make it feel natural and easy to play.

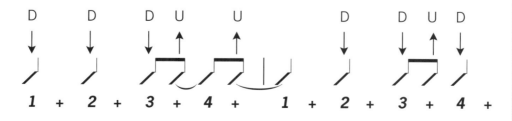

Don't You (Forget About Me)
Words & Music by Keith Forsey & Steve Schiff

Intro

‖: D Em | Em | D Em | C D :‖

Verse 1

   E   D
Won't you come see about me?
A   D
I'll be alone, dancing, you know it, baby.
   E   D
Tell me your troubles and doubts,
A   D
Giving me everything inside and out.
       E   D
And   love's strange, so real in the dark.
A   D
Think of the tender things that we were working on.
   E   D
Slow change may pull us apart
A   D
When the light gets into your heart, baby;

Chorus 1

   E   Dsus2 |Asus4 A |
   Don't you   forget about me.
Dsus2
Don't, don't, don't, don't,
   E   Dsus2 |Asus4 A | A
   Don't you   forget about me.

Bridge

C   C   G   G
Will you stand a - bove me, look my way, never love me?
D   D   A   A
Rain keeps falling, rain keeps falling   down, down, down.
C   C   G   G
Will you recog - nise me, call my name or walk on by?
D   D   A   A
Rain keeps falling, rain keeps falling   down, down, down.

Link 1

‖: D Em | Em | D Em | C D :‖

Verse 2

Don't you try and pretend,
It's my feeling we'll win in the end.
I won't harm you or touch your defences,
Vanity, insecurity.
Don't you forget about me,
I'll be alone, dancing, you know it, baby.
Going to take you apart:
I'll put us back together at heart, baby.

© COPYRIGHT 1985 MCA MUSIC (A DIVISION OF MCA INCORPORATED), USA.
UNIVERSAL/MCA MUSIC LIMITED.
ALL RIGHTS RESERVED. INTERNATIONAL COPYRIGHT SECURED.

Chorus 2 As Chorus 1

Link 2

|: Dsus²   E
     As you walk on by

Dsus² |Asus⁴   A |
   Will you call my name? _____ :||

Dsus²   E   D   A
   When you walk away,

D   E   D   A
Oh, will you walk away,

D   E   D
Will you walk on by?

A   D
Come on, call my name.

E   D   A   D
Will you call my name?   I said;

Coda

|: E   Dsus²   A   Dsus²
   La, la la la la-ah, la la la la-ah, la la la, la-la la la-la la. :||

Repeat to fade

Introduction

This song by Simple Minds will always be associated as the theme to John Hughes' era-defining movie *The Breakfast Club*, released in 1985.

Strumming

This tune was mostly played on keyboards so you have a lot of freedom to experiment with the way you play the rhythm for this song. The pattern shown below is one that I think sounds pretty good, but you should certainly experiment with it yourself and see what you think sounds cool!

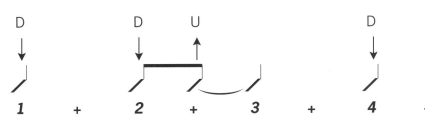

149

You Really Got Me
Words & Music by Ray Davies

Intro

F ‖: G G F G   F | G G F G   F :‖

Verse 1

| G G F G   F | G G F   G
Girl,   you really got me goin',
     F | G G F   G   F | G G F G
You got me so I don't know what I'm doin'.
F | G G F G   F | G G F   G
   Yeah,   you really got me now,
     F | G G F   G   F | G G F G
You got me so I can't sleep at night.
A A G A   G | A A G   A
Yeah,   you really got me now,
G | A A G   A   G | A A G A
You got me so I don't know what I'm doin',   now.
C | D D C D   C | D D C   D
Oh yeah,   you really got me now,
     C | D D C   D
You got me so I   can't sleep at night.

Chorus 1

C | D   D C D
You real - ly got me,
C | D   D C D
You real - ly got me,
C | D   D C D | C | (C) |
You real - ly got me.

Verse 2

See, don't ever set me free,
I always wanna be by your side.
Girl, you really got me now,
You got me so I can't sleep at night.
Yeah, you really got me now,
You got me so I don't know what I'm doin', now.
Oh yeah, you really got me now,
You got me so I can't sleep at night.

Chorus 2   As Chorus 1

Guitar solo   ‖: G G F G   F | G G F G   F :‖ *Play x4*

Verse 3   As Verse 2

Chorus 3   As Chorus 1

© COPYRIGHT 1964 EDWARD KASSNER MUSIC COMPANY LIMITED.
ALL RIGHTS RESERVED. INTERNATIONAL COPYRIGHT SECURED.

Introduction

One of the simplest but most effective riffs ever, whether heard on The Kinks original (1964) or given a whammy-bar driven makeover by Van Halen in 1978.

Riff

When the chords for a song are all power chords, it is common to describe the chords without saying '5' each time. This song is a good example: it has lots of chords, they are all power chords, and calling each chord a '5' chord simply makes it over-complicated.

To make your power chord changes fast and smooth, use the correct power chord shifting technique explained in Stage 9, lesson BC-192. It will really help you make these fast chord changes easy!

In the silences between chords it is best to keep your picking hand resting on the strings to make sure they stay quiet. If they are left open they might well ring out when you don't want them to, especially if you are using a lot of distortion and/or volume.

Here is the riff in tab in its three permutations for this song:

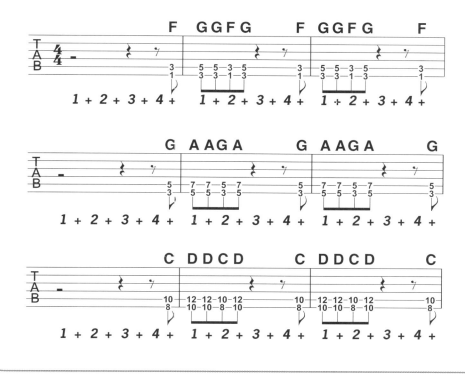

Have A Nice Day
Words & Music by Kelly Jones

Capo Fret 2

Intro

|: A Asus² A | Asus² A |
Ba-ba da, ba ba ba-da da,
Dsus²   Dsus²
Ba-ba da, ba ba ba-da da. :|

Verse 1

A Asus² A | Asus² A |
San Francisco Bay, past Pier Thirty - nine,
Dsus²
Early p.m., can't remember what time.
A Asus² A | Asus² A |
Got the waiting cab, stopped at the red light,
Dsus²
Address unsure of but it turned out just (right.)

| G | G | D | D |
right.

Verse 2

It started straight off: "Coming here is hell."
That's his first words, we asked what he meant.
He said, "Where ya from?" We told him our lot.
"When ya take a holiday is this what you want?"

Chorus 1

         A   A   Dsus²   Dsus²
|: So have a ni - ce day, have a ni - ce day, :|

Verse 3

Lie around all day, have a drink, a chase.
Yourself and tourists, yeah, that's what I hate.
He said, "We're going wrong, we've all become the same:
We dress the same ways, only our accents change."

Chorus 2 As Chorus 1

Solo

| E | E | D | D |

| E | E | D | Dm |

A Asus² A | Asus² A |
|: Ba-ba da, ba ba ba-da da,
Dsus²   Dsus²
Ba-ba da, ba ba ba-da da. :|

Verse 4

Swim in the ocean, that be my dish:
I drive around all day and kill processed fish.
It's all money-gum, no artists anymore;
You're only in it now to make more, more, more.

Chorus 2 |: As Chorus 1 :| *Repeat to fade*

© COPYRIGHT 2001 STEREOPHONICS MUSIC LIMITED.
UNIVERSAL MUSIC PUBLISHING LIMITED.
ALL RIGHTS RESERVED. INTERNATIONAL COPYRIGHT SECURED.

Introduction

Stereophonics released this song in 2001 as a single from their album *Just Enough Education To Perform*.

Singing And Playing

Many people have problems singing and playing over complex rhythm patterns. The trick is to make sure the pattern has become automatic, and to do this you just have to do it over and over again…One thing I have found that can help is to try and sing while you play the rhythm with the chords muted (just lay your fingers over the strings so when you strum you just get a click sound). Taking away the chord changes can help you get used to playing the groove and feeling of the rhythm and vocal without letting the chords and chord changes get in the way. Once you get that down you shouldn't find it too difficult to add in the chords!

 ## Strumming

The strumming pattern for this tune is very cool—a two-bar pattern that feels a little strange because you don't play on beat 1 of the second bar. It's a cool one to learn and really makes the tune sound groovy!

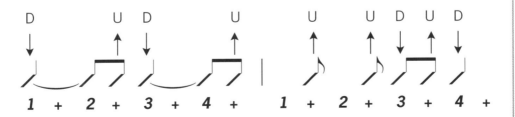

Love Is All Around

Words & Music by Reg Presley

Capo Fret 7

Intro

| G   C | D   C | G   C | D   C |

Verse 1

```
|G        Am  |C       D  |G    Am  |C  D |
 I feel it in my fingers, I feel it in my toes,
|G        Am  |C          D  |G    Am  |C  D |
 The love that's all around me, and so the feeling grows,
|G        Am |C         D  |G    Am |C  D |
 It's written on the wind, it's every - where I go,
|G        Am |C       D  |G    Am |C  D |D |
 So if you really love me, come on and let it show.
```

Chorus 1

```
         C                Am
You know I love you, I always will,
         C                G
My mind's made up by the way that I feel.
         C                    Am
There's no beginning, there'll be no end,
         Am          D          D7
'Cause on my love you can depend.
```

Verse 2

I see your face before me as I lay on my bed,
I kinda get to thinking of all the things you said.
You gave your promise to me and I gave mine to you,
I need someone beside me in everything I do.

Chorus 2

You know I love you, I always will,
My mind's made up by the way I feel.
There's no beginning, there'll be no end,
'Cause on my love you can depend.

Verse 3

It's written on the wind, it's everywhere I go.
So if you really love me, come on and let it show.
Come on and let it show.

Repeat last line to fade

© COPYRIGHT 1967 DICK JAMES MUSIC LIMITED.
UNIVERSAL/DICK JAMES MUSIC LIMITED.
ALL RIGHTS RESERVED. INTERNATIONAL COPYRIGHT SECURED.

Introduction

A hit for The Troggs in 1967, this song is probably best known for the 1992 version by Wet Wet Wet, which stayed at No. 1 for 15 weeks before being withdrawn from sale (put your capo at the 3rd fret to match that version).

Pick or fingers?

This tune can be played strummed or fingerstyle. Another cool trick you might like to play about with is to pick out four notes at random from each chord in the verses (either with a pick or your fingers). You'll be surprised how easy it is to make this sound good.

Strumming

There are many ways of playing this song that will sound cool, but the most basic one you should start with is simply playing a down, down up pattern as shown below.

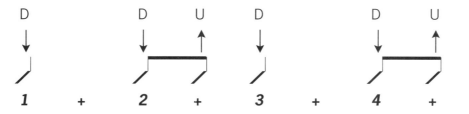

Down Under
Words & Music by Colin Hay & Ron Strykert

Capo Fret 7

Intro

| drums ‖: Em D | Em C D | Em D | Em C D :‖

Verse 1

|Em   D |Em   C D|
 Travelling in a fried-out combie
|Em   D |Em   C D|
 On a hippie trail head full of zombie.
|Em   D |Em   C   D|
 I met a strange lady,   she made me nervous
|Em   D |Em   C D|
 She took me in and gave me breakfast and she said

Chorus 1

G   D |Em C D |
 Do you come from a land down under?
G   D |Em C D |
 Where women glow and men plun - der?
G   D |Em C D
 Can't you hear, can't you hear the thunder?
|G   D |Em C D |
 You better run, you better take co - ver.

Verse 2

Buying bread from a man in Brussels,
He was six foot four and full of muscles.
I said do you speak-a my language?
He just smiled and gave me a Vegemite sandwich.
And he said:

Chorus 2

I come from a land down under,
Where beer does flow and men chunder.
Can't you hear, can't you hear the thunder?
You better run, you better take cover.

Link

‖: Em D | Em C D | Em D | Em C D :‖   *Play x3*

Verse 3

Lying in a den in Bombay,
With a slack jaw and not much to say.
I said to the man "Are you trying to tempt me?
Because I come from the land of plenty."
And he said "Oh!"

Chorus 3

Do you come from a land down under?...

Chorus 4

Living in a land down under…

© COPYRIGHT 1982 EMI SONGS AUSTRALIA PTY. LIMITED.
EMI SONGS LIMITED.
ALL RIGHTS RESERVED. INTERNATIONAL COPYRIGHT SECURED.

Introduction

The definitive Aussie anthem, first released by Men At Work in 1981...

Changing the groove

The original groove in the guitar part in this song has almost a reggae feel, with the guitar playing mostly off-beats. However, more recently Colin Hay (the singer for Men At Work and the co-writer of this song) has played it live acoustically with a much more strummy groove and it sounds great. Something to remember on your journey is to experiment with songs as you learn them—try playing fast songs slow, and slow songs fast—and you might come up with something really cool. There are many great cover versions of songs where people have made something really special by changing the feel of the original.

Strumming

Here is the off-beat feel groove which is the basis of the original track:

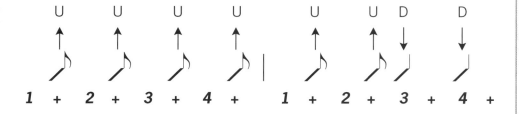

Weather With You

Words & Music by Neil Finn & Tim Finn

Intro

$\|:$ Em7 | Asus4 | Em7 | Asus4 :$\|$

Verse 1

   (Asus4)   Em7   Asus4
Walking 'round the room singing 'Stormy Weather'
        Em7   Asus4
At Fifty-Seven Mount Pleasant Street.
         Em7   Asus4
Well, it's the same room but everything's dif - ferent,
         Em7   Asus4
You can fight the sleep but not the dream.

Bridge

| Dm   C | Dm   C |
  Things ain't cookin'   in my kitchen,
 Dm   C | F
  Strange af - fliction wash over me.
| Dm   C | Dm   C |
  Julius Caesar   and the Roman Empire
 Dm   C | F   G |
  Couldn't conquer the blue sky.___

Link 1

| Em7 | Asus4 | Em7 | Asus4 |

Chorus 1

  Asus4   D
Everywhere you go you always take the weather with you.
                Asus4   D
Everywhere you go you always take the weather.
                Asus4   G
Everywhere you go you always take the weather with you.
               D | G
Everywhere you go you always take the weather,
     A | (Em7)
The weather with you.

Link 2

| Em7 | Asus4 | Em7 | Asus4 |

Verse 2

Well there's a small boat made of china,
It's going nowhere on the mantlepiece.
Well, do I lie like a lounge-room lizard,
Or do I sing like a bird released?

Chorus 2

As Chorus 1

© COPYRIGHT 1991 ROUNDHEAD MUSIC/REBEL LARYNX MUSIC, USA.
UNIVERSAL MUSIC PUBLISHING LIMITED (50%)/KOBALT MUSIC PUBLISHING LIMITED (50%).
ALL RIGHTS RESERVED. INTERNATIONAL COPYRIGHT SECURED.

| Guitar solo | ‖: Em7 | Asus4 | Em7 | Asus4 :‖ |

Chorus 3

Asus4   D
Everywhere you go you always take the weather with you.
              Asus4   D
Everywhere you go you always take the weather.
              Asus4   G
Everywhere you go you always take the weather with you.
             D   E
Everywhere you go you always take the weather,
|G   A |D
Take the weather, the weather with you.

Chorus 4

(D)
As Chorus 3

Introduction

...and the defining New Zealand anthem, released in 1991 on Crowded House's *Woodface* album.

Em7

To play Em7, play a regular Em (with 1st and 2nd fingers), and use your 4th finger on the 3rd fret of the second string. Leave it there when you change to the Asus4, moving your 1st and 2nd fingers down a string and you'll be on the right chord. This is just used in the verses. This song uses continuous strumming with various accents used to give it interest. But rather than starting with continuous strumming, a cool thing to try is to start with eight down-strums in the bar; get that grooving and then try adding in some up-strums if you think it will sound cool. If you know how the song goes it's very likely that you'll naturally start adding the up-strums in a similar way to the recording.

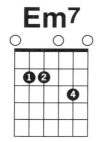
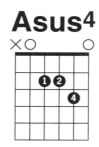

STAGE 8 BC-181—BC-189

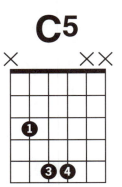

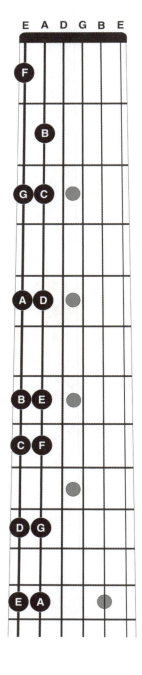

✏ Introduction

By Stage 8 we have finished off looking at power chords so you now should be using them on both fifth and sixth string root notes—so now go back and look at the tunes from the last stage and work out when you should use a fifth string root and when to use a sixth. This is something you have to learn: don't always expect to be shown or told which to use! The diagram below shows the notes on the fifth string for playing chords such as C5, shown on the left. We also look at a few different ways to play the G chord (BC-181). Again, you have to figure out which shape to use and when. It all depends on what you are playing before and after the chord, and the style of music you are playing, so try to develop the confidence to choose your grip! Don't forget to keep practising your One-Minute Changes (BC-182).

We also look at a 12-Bar blues shuffle (BC-183), so now would be a good time to go and re-visit those blues songs we covered back in Stage 5 and use that shuffle pattern with them. The new strumming we check out too is very cool: a much-used technique in many styles but most obviously folk and country. It is worth trying out on songs you have learned earlier of course; try and get a feeling for when a particular pattern is going to work. You will only develop that by trying stuff and making mistakes—don't be scared—just get in there and try it out!

We also have a couple of fingerstyle tunes (BC-184). You might find them tricky at first, but they will get better with practice and eventually seem easy. Songs in this stage such as 'Vincent' (page 168) use a type of fingerstyle where there is not a set finger-picking pattern; the pattern changes on each chord (although there are parts where a pattern appears the same in each verse). Although this sounds very complex, the idea of being free to play whatever picking pattern you fancy is also very cool. It takes a lot of practice to be able to improvise a picking pattern and sing at the same time, but it's great fun to play around with various patterns. The only important 'rule' is to make sure you play the bass note root on the beat or change of each chord.

Stage 8 Chords

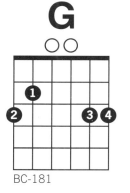
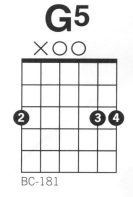
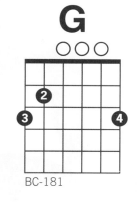

Shuffle Riff BC-183

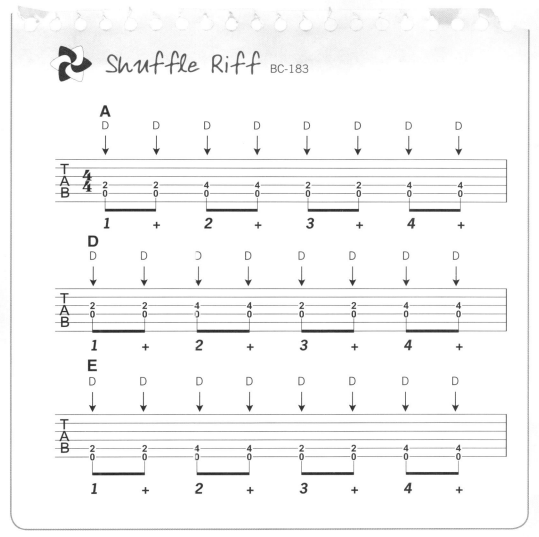

Hallelujah
Words & Music by Leonard Cohen

Verse 1
```
        C            Am
Now I've heard there was a secret chord
        C              Am
That David played, and it pleased the Lord
      F         G            C       G
But you don't really care for music, do you?
      C         |F        G    |
It goes like this: the fourth, the fifth,
        Am           F
The minor fall, the major lift,
        G        E       Am     Am
The baffled king composing Hallelujah.
```

Chorus 1
```
         F    F        Am   Am         F     F
Halle - lujah,   Halle - lujah,   Halle - lujah,
         C G C  G
Hallelu - jah.
```

Verse 2
Your faith was strong but you needed proof,
You saw her bathing on the roof:
Her beauty and the moonlight overthrew you.
She tied you to a kitchen chair,
She broke your throne, and she cut your hair
And from your lips she drew the Hallelujah.

Chorus 2   As Chorus 1

Verse 3
You say I took the name in vain,
I don't even know the name,
But if I did, well really, what's it to you?
There's a blaze of light in every word,
It doesn't matter which you heard:
The holy or the broken Hallelujah.

Chorus 3   As Chorus 1

Verse 4
I did my best, it wasn't much,
I couldn't feel, so I tried to touch.
I've told the truth, I didn't come to fool you
And even though it all went wrong
I'll stand before the Lord of Song
With nothing on my tongue but Hallelujah.

Chorus 4   As Chorus 1

© COPYRIGHT 1984 SONY/ATV MUSIC PUBLISHING.
ALL RIGHTS RESERVED. INTERNATIONAL COPYRIGHT SECURED.

Introduction

This song first appeared on Leonard Cohen's *Various Positions* album in 1984, but has become famous for a number of notable cover versions by John Cale, Jeff Buckley (you need a capo, fret 7 for this), Rufus Wainwright and KD Lang (capo fret 4). Is there another modern song with such a history?

 ## Your own Fingerstyle Pattern

Maybe now would be a fun time to make up your own fingerstyle pattern. As long as you play the bass note of the chord on beat 1, you are pretty free to pick any other notes you like, my suggestion being that you keep to six notes in a bar and use the 'normal' fingering (the three fingers pick the thinnest three strings, and the thumb plays the bass, as shown in the Beginner's Course lessons (e.g. BC-193). It's really good fun and you will learn a lot in the process!

 ## Strumming

This song is played with a 6/8 feel, meaning that there are two beats in a bar and each beat is divided into three, so either play it with just two strums per bar, or with six. If you use six, then play them all as down-strums and if you fancy it, experiment with adding a few up-strums in between.

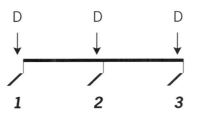 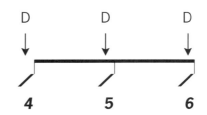

Fast Car

Words & Music by Tracy Chapman

Capo Fret 2

Play fingerstyle riff (shown opposite) in Verses

Verse 1
You got a fast car, I want a ticket to anywhere.
Maybe we make a deal, maybe together we can get somewhere.
Any place is better.
Starting from zero, got nothing to lose.
Maybe we'll make something, Me myself, I got nothing to prove.

Verse 2
You got a fast car, I got a plan to get us out of here:
I been working at the convenience store,
Managed to save just a little bit of money.
Won't have to drive too far just 'cross the border and into the city,
You and I can both get jobs and finally see what it means to be living.

Verse 3
You see my old man's got a problem:
He live with the bottle, that's the way it is.
He says his body's too old for working,
His body's too young to look like his.
My mama went off and left him,
She wanted more from life than he could give,
I said, "Somebody's got to take care of him."
So I quit school and that's what I did.

Verse 4
You got a fast car, but is it fast enough so we can fly away?
We gotta make a decision:
Leave tonight or live and die this way.

Chorus 1
          C
I remember when we were driving, driving in your car,
 G
The speed so fast I felt like I was drunk,
Em
  City lights lay out before us
     D
And your arm felt nice wrapped 'round my shoulder.
|**C** **Em** |**D** |
And I ____had a feeling that I belonged
|**C** **Em** |**D** |**C**   **D** |
And I ____ had a feeling I could be someone, be someone, be someone.

Verse 5
You got a fast car, and we go cruising to entertain ourselves;
You still ain't got a job and I work in a market as a checkout girl.
I know things will get better: you'll find work and I'll get promoted,
We'll move out of the shelter buy a bigger house and live in the suburbs.

Chorus 2
As Chorus 1

© COPYRIGHT 1987 SBK APRIL MUSIC INCORPORATED/PURPLE RABBIT MUSIC, USA.
EMI SONGS LIMITED.
ALL RIGHTS RESERVED. INTERNATIONAL COPYRIGHT SECURED.

Verse 6 You got a fast car and I got a job that pays all our bills.
You stay out drinking late at the bar,
See more of your friends than you do of your kids.
I'd always hoped for better,
Thought maybe together you and me would find it,
I got no plans I ain't going nowhere,
So take your fast car and keep on driving.

Chorus 3 As Chorus 1

Verse 7 You got a fast car but is it fast enough so you can fly away?
You gotta make a decision: leave tonight or live and die this way.

Tracy Chapman famously broke into public consciousness by playing this and other songs while filling in time during a technical hitch at the 1988 Nelson Mandela birthday concert at Wembley Stadium.

Playing slowly and in time!

The best way to get fingerstyle patterns sounding great is to play them really slowly and get the timing and pattern perfect before speeding up. Otherwise you can actually end up learning to play your mistakes; take your time in the early stages and make 100% sure that you get the right notes in the right order. It also helps to be aware of which notes are played together and which are played on their own!

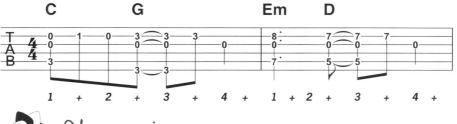

Strumming

Most of this tune is fingerstyle but this 'pumping 8s' strumming is used from Chorus 1:

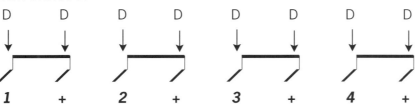

Fields Of Gold
Words & Music by Sting

Capo Fret 2

Intro

|: Am | Am | Am | Am :|

Verse 1

        Asus²   **F**
You'll re - member me when the west wind moves
  F   **C**
U - pon the fields of barley.
        Asus² |**F**   **C** |
You'll for - get the sun in his jealous sky
|**F** **G** |**Am** | **Am F** |**C** |**C** |
As we walk in fields of gold.
        Asus²   **F**
So she took her love for to gaze a while
  F   **C**
U - pon the fields of barley.
        Asus² |**F**   **C** |
In his arms she fell as her hair came down
|**F** **G** |**C**
Among   the fields of gold.

Verse 2

Will you stay with me, will you be my love
Among the fields of barley?
We'll forget the sun in his jealous sky
As we lie in fields of gold.
See the west wind move like a lover so,
Upon the fields of barley.
Feel her body rise when you kiss her mouth,
Among the fields of gold.

Middle

F   **C**
  I never made promises lightly,
F   **C**
  And there have been some that I've broken,
F   **C**
  But I swear in the days still left
|**F** **G** |**C**
We'll walk   in fields of gold,
|**F** **G** |**C** |**C** |
We'll walk in fields of gold.

Instrumental

| Asus² | F | F | C |
| Asus² | F C | F G | C |

© COPYRIGHT 1992 STEERPIKE LIMITED/STEERPIKE (OVERSEAS) LIMITED/EMI MUSIC PUBLISHING LIMITED.
ALL RIGHTS RESERVED. INTERNATIONAL COPYRIGHT SECURED.

Verse 3   Many years have passed since those summer days
Among the fields of barley.
See the children run as the sun goes down
Among the fields of gold.
You'll remember me when the west wind moves
Upon the fields of barley.
You can tell the sun in his jealous sky
When we walked in fields of gold,
When we walked in fields of gold,
When we walked in fields of gold.

 Introduction

Originally recorded on Sting's *Ten Summoner's Tales* in 1993, this song was to become associated with Eva Cassidy, whose version became posthumously famous.

 Nails or flesh?

When you play fingerstyle you can use your fingernails or the flesh of your fingertips, but you shouldn't combine both. If you have some nails long and some short then some notes will come out louder than others and it will sound strange. If you have trouble growing your nails there are things you can apply to make them stronger, or you can get fake nails (acrylic or gel) which work great but might get you strange looks…

 Strumming

This song doesn't have a proper strumming pattern but this one sounds cool and has the right groove. It's fun to experiment with fingerstyle in this song too.

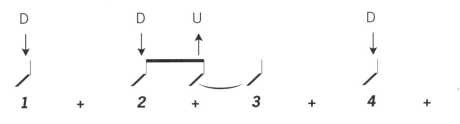

Vincent

Words & Music by Don McLean

Verse 1

    N.C. |**G**   **C**|
Starry, starry night,
 G |**Am**   **Asus²**|
   Paint your palette blue and grey,
Am   **C**
   Look out on a summer's day,
   D7   **G**
With eyes that know the darkness in my soul.
         G   **C**
Shadows on the hills,
 G |**Am**   **Asus²**|
   Sketch the trees and the daffodils,
Am   **C**
   Catch the breeze and the winter chills,
 D7 |**G** **C**|
In colours on the snowy linen land.

Chorus 1

   G   **Am**
   Now I under - stand
D7   **G**
   What you tried to say to me,
Em   **Am**
   How you suffered for your sanity
D7   **Em**
   How you tried to set them free.
              A7 |**Am**
They would not listen, they did not know how,
 D7 |**G** **G**
Per - haps they'll listen now.

Verse 2

Starry, starry night,
Flaming flowers that brightly blaze,
Swirling clouds in violet haze,
Reflect in Vincent's eyes of china blue.
Colours changing hue,
Morning fields of amber grain,
Weathered faces lined in pain,
Are soothed beneath the artist's loving hand.

Chorus 2 As Chorus 1

Middle

            Am
For they could not love you,
 D7   **G**
   Still your love was true;
Em   **Am**
   And when no hope was left inside
   Cm
On that starry, starry night

© COPYRIGHT 1971 MAYDAY MUSIC, USA.
UNIVERSAL/MCA MUSIC LIMITED.
ALL RIGHTS RESERVED. INTERNATIONAL COPYRIGHT SECURED.

```
         |G          Fmaj7      |E
```
You took your life as lovers often do;
```
            Asus2
```
But I could have told you Vincent
```
            C                              D7        |G    C   |G
```
This world was never meant for one as beautiful as you.

Verse 3 Starry, starry night,
Portraits hung in empty halls,
Frameless heads on nameless walls,
With eyes that watch the world and can't forget.
Like the strangers that you've met,
The raggec men in ragged clothes,
The silver thorn of bloody rose,
Lie crushed and broken on the virgin snow.

Chorus 3 Now I think I know
What you tried to say to me,
And how you suffered for your sanity,
How you tried to set them free.
They woulc not listen, they're not listening still,
Perhaps they never will.

The 'Cheating' Cm chord

This Don McLean song has a Cm chord in the middle section. For now, you can play this using an Am shape, up three frets, taking care only to play the three strings shown:

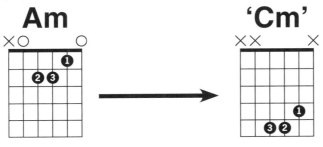

Strumming

This song is really a fingerstyle tune, but simple strumming will work too:

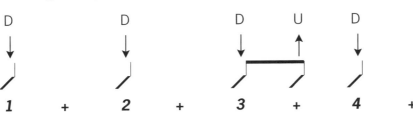

Wonderwall

Words & Music by Noel Gallagher

Capo Fret 2

Intro   ‖: Em7 G | Dsus4 | A7sus4 | Em7 G | Dsus4 | A7sus4 :‖

Verse 1
|Em7   G
Today is gonna be the day
         |Dsus4   A7sus4|
That they're gonna throw it back to you,
Em7   G
By now you should have somehow
     |Dsus4   A7sus4|
Realised what you gotta do.
Em7   G |Dsus4   A7sus4
I don't believe that anybody feels the way I do
          |Cadd9 Dsus4 | A7sus4
About you now.

Verse 2
Back beat, the word is on the street, that the fire in your heart is out,
I'm sure you've heard it all before, but you never really had a doubt.
I don't believe that anybody feels the way I do,
    |Em7   G |Dsus4   A7sus4
about you now.

Bridge 1
     |C   D |Em
And all the roads we have to walk are winding,
     |C   D |Em
And all the lights that lead us there are blinding,
|C   D |G   D   Em
There are many things that I would like to say to you
          |A7sus4   A7sus4
But I don't know how.

Chorus 1
          |Cadd9   Em7 | G
Because maybe,
         Em7 |Cadd9   Em7 | G
You're gonna be the one that saves me,
    Em7 |Cadd9 Em7 | G
And after all,
          Em7 |Cadd9 Em7 | G Em7 | N.C. A7sus4 |
You're my wonderwall.

Verse 3
Today was gonna be the day,
But they'll never throw it back at you,
By now you should have somehow
Realised what you're not to do.
I don't believe that anybody feels the way I do
About you now.

Bridge 2   As Bridge 1

Chorus 2   As Chorus 2 *(repeat to end)*

© COPYRIGHT 1995 CREATION SONGS LIMITED/OASIS MUSIC (GB).
SONY/ATV MUSIC PUBLISHING.
ALL RIGHTS RESERVED. INTERNATIONAL COPYRIGHT SECURED.

Introduction

One of the songs that defined the Britpop era, first released in 1995.

New Chords

At first glance it might seem that there are lots of chords that you have not learned yet in this song, but there is a little trick to these chords that makes it all simple. What we have here are pretty normal chords, but you have to leave your 3rd and 4th fingers down on strings 1 and 2 at the 3rd fret for the whole song. When you do that Em becomes Em7, A becomes A7sus4, C becomes Cadd9, etc. Of course you are going to need to change some fingering for the chords—and they sound a bit different—but it's a cool trick.

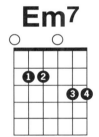
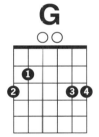
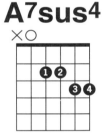
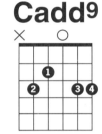

Strumming

The strumming played on the recording of this tune is pretty tricky for a beginner, but lots of people like having a go at it anyhow. So you can either simplify the strumming (just one strum on each beat sounds pretty cool) or listen closely to the recording and have a go at the proper strumming. I warn you—it is pretty hard going for a beginner, and will take a lot of effort—but it will be worth it when you get it because it's a party favourite!

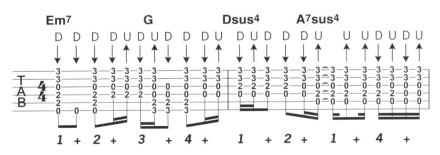

Polly
Words & Music by Kurt Cobain

Intro

‖: Em   G | D   C :‖

Verse 1

| Em G | D   C |
Polly wants a cracker
| Em G | D   C |
I think I should get off her first
| Em G | D   C |
I think she wants some water
| Em G | D   C |
To put out the blow torch

Chorus 1

| D C | G   B♭ |
It isn't me   we have some seed
| D C | G   B♭ |
Let me clip   dirty wings
| D C | G   B♭ |
Let me take a ride   cut yourself
| D C | G   B♭ |
Want some help   please myself
| D C | G   B♭ |
I've got some rope   you have been told
| D C | G   B♭ |
Promise you   I've been true
| D C | G   B♭ |
Let me take a ride cut yourself
| D C | G   B♭ |
I want some help   please myself

Verse 2

Polly wants a cracker
Maybe she would like some food
She asked me to untie her
A chase would be nice for a few

Chorus 2   As Chorus 1

Verse 3

Polly says her back hurts
And she's just as bored as me
She caught me off my guard
It amazes me, the will of instinct

Chorus 3   As Chorus 1

© COPYRIGHT 1991 THE END OF MUSIC/PRIMARY WAVE TUNES, USA.
EMI VIRGIN MUSIC LIMITED.
ALL RIGHTS RESERVED. INTERNATIONAL COPYRIGHT SECURED.

Introduction

This album track from Nirvana's *Nevermind* was a natural choice for the band's *Unplugged* set in 1995.

Power Chords

Power chords work great on acoustic guitar too as you can hear in this tune. Don't be too aggressive with them because on acoustic they will get all scratchy and rattle, so be a little more delicate. This song sounds great on electric with a clean sound too.

Strumming

The strumming in this tune really makes it sound right and getting the chord changes in the right place is very important. Kurt Cobain was a bit slow making the chord changes so the 'ands' are usually just open strings and the chords land on the beat. This makes it feel like a push, but it's not really!

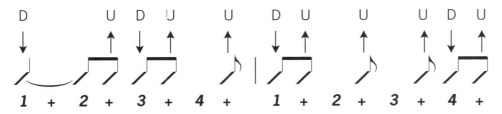

Molly's Chambers
Words & Music by Caleb Followill, Nathan Followill & Angelo Petraglia

Verse 1

(with riff throughout)
Free is all that she could bleed
That's why'll she'll never stay
White bare naked in the night
And lookin' for some play.
Just another girl that wants to rule the world
Any time or place,
And when she gets into your head
You know she's there to stay.

Chorus 1

B^5
   You want it
A^5
   She's got it
with riff x2
Molly's chamber's gonna change your mind
B^5
   She's got your,
D^5
   Your pistol.
with riff x2
Molly's chamber's gonna change your mind
with riff x2
Molly's chamber's gonna change your mind.

Verse 2

(with riff throughout)
Slow, she's burnin' in your soul
With whispers in your ear.
It's okay I'll give it anyway
Just get me outta here.
You'll plead, you'll get down on your knees
For just another taste,
And when you think she's let you in
That's when she fades away.

Chorus 2   As Chorus 1

Guitar solo

| B^5 D^5 | $F\sharp^5$ | B^5 D^5 | $F\sharp^5$ |
| B^5 D^5 | $F\sharp^5$ | A^5 | B^5 |

Chorus 3   As Chorus 1

© COPYRIGHT 2003 MUSIC OF WINDSWEPT/GREEN WAGON MUSIC/UNIVERSAL POLYGRAM INTERNATIONAL/
SOUTHSIDE INDEPENDENT MUSIC PUBLISHING, USA.
BUG MUSIC (WINDSWEPT ACCOUNT) (55.55%)/UNIVERSAL MUSIC PUBLISHING LIMITED (33.34%)
WARNER/CHAPPELL NORTH AMERICA LIMITED (11.11%).
ALL RIGHTS RESERVED. INTERNATIONAL COPYRIGHT SECURED.

Introduction

This song is taken from the first Kings of Leon album, *Youth And Young Manhood* (2003).

 ## Riff Variations

There is a very subtle difference in the way this riff is played between the intro, instrumental bit and chorus, and the verses. The intro has the chord played on beat 2, but in the verses the chord played on beat 1 is tied over beat 2, so the next strum is on the 'and' after '2'.

Intro/Chorus:

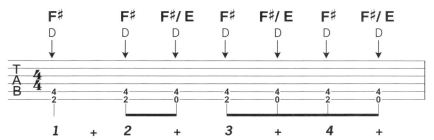

Verse:

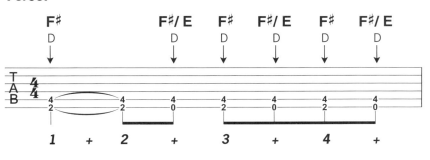

The Sound Of Silence
Words & Music by Paul Simon

Capo Fret **6**

Verse 1
   Asus²   **G**
Hello, darkness, my old friend,
 G   **Asus²**
I've come to talk with you a - gain,
|**Asus²**   **C** |**F**   **C** |
Because a vision softly creeping
C |$\frac{2}{4}$**F** |$\frac{4}{4}$**C**
Left its seeds while I was sleeping
       F   **F**   **C**
And the vision that was planted in my brain
    |**C**   **Am**|
Still re - mains
$\frac{2}{4}$**C** |$\frac{4}{4}$**G**   **Asus²**
  Within the sound of silence.

Verse 2
In restless dreams I walked alone
Narrow streets of cobblestone.
Beneath the halo of a street lamp
I turned my collar to the cold and damp
When my eyes were stabbed
By the flash of a neon light
That split the night
And touched the sound of silence.

Verse 3
And in the naked light I saw
Ten thousand people, maybe more:
People talking without speaking,
People hearing without listening,
People writing songs that voices never share
And no-one dare
Disturb the sound of silence.

Verse 4
"Fools," said I, "You do not know
Silence like a cancer grows.
Hear my words that I might teach you,
Take my arms that I might reach you."
But my words like silent raindrops fell,
And echoed in the wells of silence.

Verse 5
And the people bowed and prayed
To the neon god they made.
And the sign flashed out its warning
In the words that it was forming,
And the sign said, "The words of the prophets
Are written on the subway walls
And tenement halls,
And whispered in the sounds of silence."

© COPYRIGHT 1964 PAUL SIMON MUSIC, USA.
ALL RIGHTS RESERVED. INTERNATIONAL COPYRIGHT SECURED.

Introduction

This Simon & Garfunkel classic was written in the aftermath of the assassination of President John F. Kennedy in 1963, capturing the grief of a nation.

Counting the Beats

As you'll see, there are some 2/4 bars in the verses of this song. However, the structure is a little different for some of the other verses. Listen carefully to the original song, and you'll pick up on these variations in the bar structure.

After the first verse, you should play Am instead of Asus2. Between the C and Am chords you could try a run down on the fifth string, adding the note B (2nd fret) to smoothly connect the two.

Picking and Strumming

The original finger-picking pattern for this song has an alternating bass part which is hard for a beginner player so I have simplified it to this pattern which will sound very similar. Keep your fingers on the same string throughout, but make sure the thumb plays the root note (it will be moving between the sixth, fifth and fourth strings).

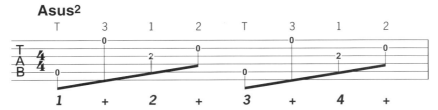

Switch to this strumming from the second verse onwards. Usually, you would only play the thinnest strings on the up-strums, but in this song it will sound great with a full sound using all the strings on all strums.

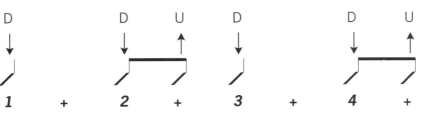

All The Small Things

Words & Music by Mark Hoppus & Thomas Delonge

Intro

G F ‖: C | F | G | G F :‖

Verse 1

```
  C         G           F          G
All the  small things,  true care,  truth brings.
  C         G           F          G
I'll take  one lift,    your ride,  best trip.
  C         G           F          G
Always   I know   you'll be   at my show
  C         G           F          G
Watching,   waiting,   commis - erating.
```

Chorus 1

```
  C              (C)           (G)
Say it ain't so, I will not go,
                   (F)
Turn the lights off, carry me home.

  C                         C
Na, na, na, na, na na, na na na na.
  G                         F
Na, na, na, na, na na, na na na na.
  C                         C
Na, na, na, na, na na, na na na na.
  G                         F
Na, na, na, na, na na, na na na na.
```

Link

‖: C | F C | G | G F :‖

Verse 2

Late night, come home,
Work sucks, I know.
She left me roses by the stairs,
Surprises let me know she cares.

Chorus 2

As Chorus 1

Link

‖: C | C | F | G :‖ Play x4

Outro

Say it ain't so, I will not go,
Turn the lights off, carry me home.
Keep your head still, I'll be your thrill,
The night will go on, my little windmill.
Say it ain't so, I will not go,
Turn the lights off, carry me home.
Keep your head still, I'll be your thrill,
The night will go on, the night will go on, my little windmill.

© COPYRIGHT 1999 FUN WITH GOATS/EMI APRIL MUSIC INCORPORATED, USA.
EMI MUSIC PUBLISHING LIMITED.
ALL RIGHTS RESERVED. INTERNATIONAL COPYRIGHT SECURED.

Introduction

Power punk pop perfection from Blink-182. Three chords are all you need!

Letting chords ring out

Make extra sure you have all the open strings carefully muted before you go for the big sustained chords in the first half of the chorus. You're only going to hit those notes once and let them ring out (the 'say it ain't so…' bit in each verse) so you need to hit them quite hard to keep them sustaining. The last thing you want is the open strings ringing out and making it sound messy!

Strumming

This one sounds best with all down-strums most of the way through. Listen to the track and try and pick up the accent patterns.

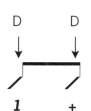
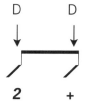
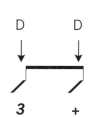
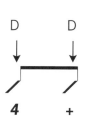

Pretty Fly (For A White Guy)

Words & Music by Thomas Allen, Harold Brown, Jerry Goldstein, Morris Dickerson, Le Roy Lonnie Jordan, Charles Miller, Lee Oskar, Howard Scott & Bryan Holland

Intro

N.C.
Gunter, gleiben, glauchen, globen.
Give it to me baby, uh huh, uh huh. *(x3)*
And all the girlies say I'm pretty fly for a white guy.

Riff

‖: B5   F♯5   A5 | B5   E5   D5 :‖ *Play x3*

B5   F♯   A5   B5   N.C.
Uno, dos, tres, cuatro, cin - co, cinco, seís.

Verse 1

        B5
You know it's kinda hard just to get along today,
Our subject isn't cool, but he thinks it anyway.
He may not have a clue and he may not have style,
But everything he lacks, well, he makes up in denial.

Chorus 1

        B5   F5 F♯5   F5 F♯5   B5   F5   F♯5
So don't debate,   'cause he's a   player straight
         F5 F♯5 D5   A5   D5   E5   D5
And ba - by   you know he really doesn't get it any - way.
     A5   B5   F5 F♯5 F5 F♯5   B5   F5   F♯5
He's gonna play the field,   he's gon - na   keep it real,
       F5 F♯5 D5   A5   D5   E5   D5 E5 F5
But not for   you, no way,   for you no   way.
E5 D5 B5   F5 F♯5   F5 F♯5   B5   F5   F♯5
So if you don't break,   just ov - er   compensate,
       F5 F♯5 D5   A5   D5   E5   D5   A5
At least that you know you can always go on Ricki Lake.
   G5   D5   G5   A5   E5   A5
   The world needs wanna - bes, ah,
B5   F♯5   F5 E5 B5 D5   E5   B5
   Come on   and do the brand new thing.

Link

w/riff
Give it to me baby, uh huh, uh huh. *(x3)*
And all the girlies say I'm pretty fly for a white guy.

Verse 2

        B
He needs some cool tunes, not just any will suffice,
But they didn't have Ice Cube so he bought Vanilla Ice.
Now cruising in his Pinto, he sees homies as he pass,
But if he looks twice, they're gonna kick his lily ass.

Chorus 2

As Chorus 1

© COPYRIGHT 1998 GAMETE MUSIC INCORPORATED/UNDERACHIEVER MUSIC, USA.
HAL LEONARD CORPORATION.
ALL RIGHTS RESERVED. INTERNATIONAL COPYRIGHT SECURED.

Verse 3
Now he's getting a tattoo yeah, he's getting ink done,
He asks for a thirteen, but they drew a thirty-one.
Friends say he's trying too hard and he's not quite hip,
But in his own mind he's the, he's the dopest trick.

Link 3
Give it to me baby, uh huh, uh huh. (x3)
Uno, dos, tres, cuatro, cinco, cinco, seís.

Chorus 3
So don't debate, 'cause he's a player straight
And baby you know he really doesn't get it anyway.
He's gonna play the field, he's gonna keep it real,
But not for you, no way, for you no way.
So if you don't break, just over compensate,
At least that you know you can always go on Ricki Lake.
The world needs wannabes, ah,
The world loves wannabes, ah,
Let's get some more wannabes, ah,
Come on and do the brand new thing.

 ## Introduction
Wannabe-baiting fun from The Offspring from their 1998 opus *Americana*.

Fast Power Chord Riffing

This one has a LOT of fast chord changes and I usually give this song out as a tester to make sure students have the power chords sounding really good and clean. Make sure you practise it slowly and carefully and get it right at a slow tempo before you try and speed it up.

'Chips'

There are not strumming patterns *per se* in this song—it's more riff based—so you need to get your ears on and listen to it a bunch of times to pick up the right rhythm for the riffs and chords. In the verses it uses 'chips', playing the thinnest two strings at the 7th fret, as follows:

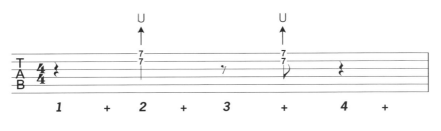

STAGE 9 BC-191—BC-199

 ## Introduction

Well we are nearly there! Hopefully you are feeling confident with it all—we have a few new things to check out in Stage 9 and then we just need to consolidate what we've learnt.

Slash chords (which have nothing to do with Guns n' Roses…) are really easy but many people get confused by their names. You use them when the chord and the bass note are different. The letter before the slash is the chord, and the letter after it is the bass note. You'll find the most accessible 'slash' chords on the next page—make sure you learn them!

We now have some fingerstyle patterns that you can play about with. Don't think that you can only use them on songs that happen to use them on the original record. Songs we looked at earlier like 'Killing Me Softly…' (page 74) will sound lovely with fingerstyle. In fact, most ballads (slow songs) will sound great! So go and try them out.

You might also like to revise those blues songs we've learned if you have a jam buddy and want to start improvising. You should also try using those 12-Bar Variations (BC-194) on them too; they will sound great and if you have been listening to some blues (as recommended) then you will certainly be familiar with how they sound. Now it's time to apply them!

 ## Stage 9: Your notes

Stage 9 Chords

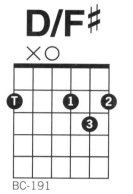
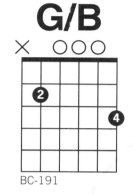
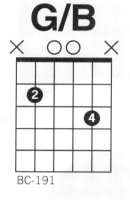
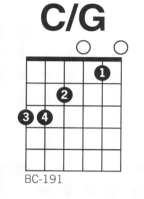

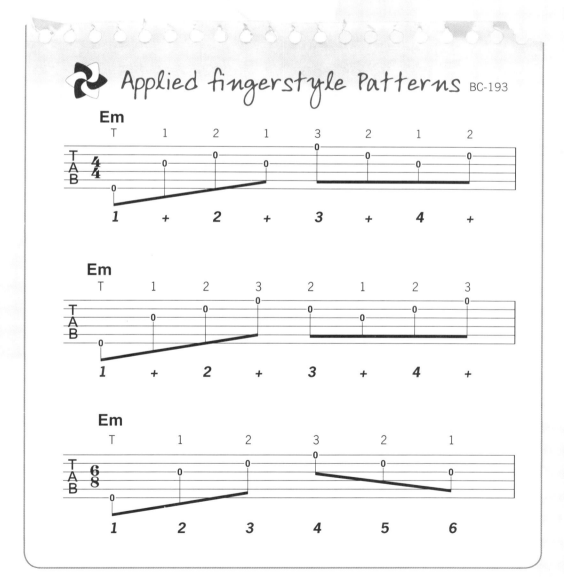

Applied Fingerstyle Patterns BC-193

Better Be Home Soon
Words & Music by Neil Finn

Verse 1
```
C              Am
Somewhere deep in - side
           Em7        | G   F |
Something's got a hold on you
C                 Am
And it's pushing me a - side
               Em7   G
See it stretch on for - ever
```

Chorus 1
```
              C   C7
I know I'm right
                       F        F
For the first time in my life
         G        G
That's why I tell you
                     C       G
You'd better be home soon
```

Verse 2
Stripping back the coats
Of lies and deception
Back to nothingness
Like a week in the desert

Chorus 2
I know I'm right
For the first time in my life
That's why I tell you
```
                     C       C/B
You'd better be home soon
```

Bridge
```
B♭         D                    G
So don't say no, don't say nothing's wrong
B♭                  A7              D
'Cause when you get back home maybe I'll be gone
```

Instr.
```
| C    | Am   | Em   | G    |
| C    | Am   | Em   |      |
| F    | F    | B♭   | B♭   |
```

Verse 3
It would cause me pain, if we were to end it
But I could start again, you can depend on it

Chorus 3
I know I'm right, for the first time in my life
```
         G        G                   Am    D
That's why I tell you,   you'd better be home soon
             F    G
That's why I tell you,   you'd better be home soon
```

© COPYRIGHT 1988 ROUNDHEAD MUSIC, USA.
UNIVERSAL MUSIC PUBLISHING LIMITED.
ALL RIGHTS RESERVED. INTERNATIONAL COPYRIGHT SECURED.

Introduction

This Crowded House song was released as a single in 1988.

 ### Power Chord Cheats

There is one B♭ chord in this song which is a good example of where you can use a power chord as a substitute for a chord that you might not yet know. Using power chords to replace barre chords when you don't know them or can't yet play them is fine for now, but soon as you start the Intermediate Method you should work in your barre chords where you can.

B♭5

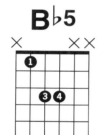

Strumming

There are many different patterns used in this song but the one shown will work well through the whole thing:

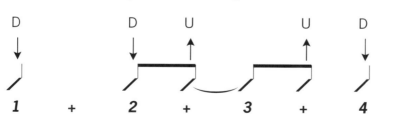

Have You Ever Seen The Rain
Words & Music by John C. Fogerty

Intro |Am |F |C |G |C |C |

Verse 1
```
    C              C
Someone told me long ago
    C             C          G
There's a calm be - fore the storm, I know
         G          C       C
And it's been coming for some time
    C            C
When it's over, so they say
   C      C        G
It'll rain a sunny day, I know
G              C    C
Shining down like water
```

Chorus 1
```
  F       G
  I wanna know
    |C    C/B  |Am    Am7/G|
Have you ever seen the rain
  F       G
  I wanna know
    |C    C/B  |Am    Am7/G|
Have you ever seen the rain
  F       G           C   C
  Coming down on a sunny day
```

Verse 2
Yesterday and days before
Sun is cold and rain is hard, I know
Been that way for all my time
Until forever on it goes
Thru' the circle fast and slow, I know
And it can't stop, I wonder

Chorus 2 As Chorus 1 *(Repeat)*

© COPYRIGHT 1970 PRESTIGE MUSIC LIMITED.
ALL RIGHTS RESERVED. INTERNATIONAL COPYRIGHT SECURED.

Introduction

This song was released by Creedence Clearwater Revival in 1970.

 Chorus bass line

There is a lovely descending bass line in the chorus of this tune. Start with a C chord. Then to play C/B just remove your 2nd and 3rd fingers and put your 3rd finger back down on the note B (fifth string, 2nd fret) and make sure the underneath of the finger mutes the fourth string (this will probably happen naturally). Next you play Am, and then simply lift off your 3rd finger and place it on the note G (6th string, 3rd fret) to get the Am7/G. It might seem hard at first, but it won't after a little practice and it'll sound great!

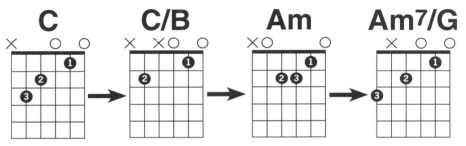

 Strumming

This is a very, very cool rhythm pattern and is very commonly used for songs in this style.

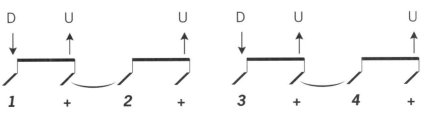

Wherever You Will Go
Words & Music by Aaron Kamin & Alex Band

Capo Fret 2

Verse 1
(with riff)
So lately, I've been wonderin'
Who will be there to take my place
When I'm gone, you'll need love
To light the shadows on your face
If a great wave shall fall
It'll fall upon us all
And between the sand and stone
Could you make it on your own.

Chorus 1
```
         C        G         Am           F            C
   If I could, then I would    I'll go wherever you will go
            G         Am           F            C
Way up high or down low    I'll go wherever you will go.
```

Verse 2
(with riff)
And maybe, I'll find out
A way to make it back someday
To watch you, to guide you
Through the darkest of your days
If a great wave shall fall
It'll fall upon us all
Well I hope there's someone out there
Who can bring me back to you.

Chorus 2
```
         C        G         Am           F            C
   If I could, then I would    I'll go wherever you will go
            G         Am           F            Am
Way up high or down low    I'll go wherever you will go.
```

Bridge
```
F                 G
Run away with my heart
Em                Am
Run away with my hope
F                 G       Em
Run away with my love.
```

Verse 3
(with riff)
I know now, just quite how
My life and love might still go on
In your heart, in your mind
I'll stay with you for all of time.

Chorus 3   As Chorus 1

Chorus 4
If I could turn back time, I'll go wherever you will go
If I could make you mine, I'll go wherever you will go.

© COPYRIGHT 2001 ALEX BAND MUSIC/AMEDEO MUSIC, USA.
UNIVERSAL MUSIC PUBLISHING MGB LIMITED.
ALL RIGHTS RESERVED. INTERNATIONAL COPYRIGHT SECURED.

Introduction

The Calling's big hit from 2001.

Riff

Getting the picking right for this riff is going to make it sound just like the original and it's not too hard to play. The original was probably played with a pick (plectrum), but fingerstyle will work as well—fingering is shown above the tab below. The note F (1st fret on the sixth string) is played with your thumb which can be tricky at first. Just take it slow, get it right and you will learn it in no time.

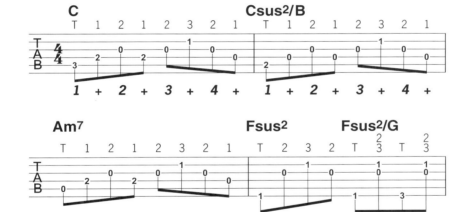

Strumming

Play the riff above in the verses and use this strumming pattern in the choruses:

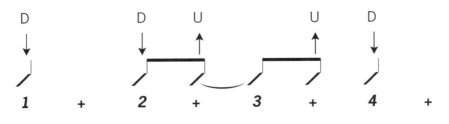

American Pie
Words & Music by Don McLean

Intro

```
        |G    D/F#|Em      Am            C
         A long, long  time ago I can still remember
                      Em                    D
         How that music used to make me smile.
        |G       D/F#|Em         Am                C
         And I knew if I had my chance that I could make those people dance
           Em         C           D         D
         And maybe they'd be happy for a while.
         Em          Am             Em           Am
            But February made me shiver   with ev'ry paper I'd deliver,
        |C      G/B  |Am          C                 D
         Bad news on the doorstep, I couldn't take one more step.
        |G       D/F#|Em            C          D
         I can't remember if I cried when I read about his widowed bride.
        |G       D/F#   |Em              C    D   G    G
         And something touched me deep inside the day the music died. So....
```

Chorus 1

```
         G    C       |G        D
         Bye-bye, Miss American Pie,
             |G      C          |G          D
         Drove my Chevy to the levee but the levee was dry.
             |G      C           |G         D
         And them good old boys were drinkin' whiskey and rye,
            |Em                   A7
         Singin' this'll be the day that I die.
         Em                D7    D7
         This'll be the day that I die.
```

Verse 1

```
         G                Am
            Did you write the book of love
                   C          Am        Em        D       D
         And do you have faith in God above,   if the Bible tells you so?
            |G       D/F#|Em          Am             C
         Now do you believe in rock and roll, can music save your mortal soul,
            Em        A7          D             D
         And  can you teach me how to dance real slow?
            Em           D            Em              D
         Well I know that you're in love with him 'cause I__ saw you dancin' in the gym.
            |C      G/B   |Am        C                D7
         You both kicked off your shoes, man I dig those rhythm and blues.
            |G       D/F#|Em             Am                 C
         I was a lonely teenage broncin' buck with a pink carnation and a pickup truck.
            |G       D/F#|Em        C    D7   |G   C|
         But I knew I was out of luck the day the music died.
         G      D       |
         I started singing....
```

© COPYRIGHT 1971 MAYDAY MUSIC, USA.
UNIVERSAL/MCA MUSIC LIMITED.
ALL RIGHTS RESERVED. INTERNATIONAL COPYRIGHT SECURED.

Verse 2
Now, for ten years we've been on our own
And moss grows fat on a rolling stone
But that's not how it used to be.
When the jester sang for the King and Queen
In a coat he borrowed from James Dean,
And a voice that came from you and me.
Oh, and while the King was looking down
The jester stole his thorny crown,
The courtroom was adjourned,
No verdict was returned.
And while Lennon read a book on Marx
The quartet practiced in the park,
And we sang dirges in the dark
The day the music died. We were singing....

Verse 3
Helter-skelter in a summer swelter,
The Byrds flew off with a fallout shelter.
Eight miles high and fallin' fast,
It landed foul out on the grass,
The players tried for a forward pass
With the jester on the sidelines in a cast.
Now the half-time air was sweet perfume
While the sergeants played a marching tune.
We all got up to dance, oh,
But we never got the chance.
'Cause the players tried to take the field,
The marching band refused to yield,
Do you recall what was revealed
The day the music died? We started singin'....

Verse 4
Oh, and there we were all in one place,
A generation lost in space
With no time left to start again.
So come on, Jack be nimble, Jack be quick,
Jack Flash sat on a candlestick,
'Cause fire is the devil's only friend.
Oh, and as I watched him on the stage
My hands were clenched in fists of rage.
No angel born in hell
Could break that Satan's spell.
And as the flames climbed high into the night
To light the sacrificial rite,
I saw Satan laughing with delight,
The day the music died. He was singin'....

Verse 5
I met a girl who sang the blues
And I asked her for some happy news,
But she just smiled and turned away.
I went down to the sacred store
Where I'd heard the music years before
But the man there said the music wouldn't play.
And in the streets the children screamed,
The lovers cried and the poets dreamed
But not a word was spoken,
The church bells all were broken.
And the three men I admire most,
The Father, Son and the Holy Ghost,
They caught the last train for the coast,
The day the music died. And they were singin'....

 ## Introduction
Originally released in 1971 on the album of the same name, this song is full of cryptic allusions to figures and events of the time.

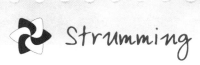

The first part of this song is played quite freely, where you strum the chords relative to the singing and you don't really have to worry about it being in time. Once you hit the chorus though it should have a steady beat for the rest of the tune.

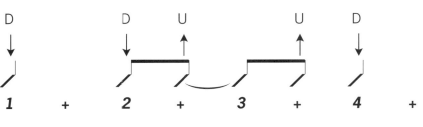

Redemption Song
Words & Music by Bob Marley

Verse 1

```
     G              Em
Old pirates yes they rob I,
|C         G/B      |Am
Sold I to the merchant ships,
 G              Em
  Minutes after they took I
|C         G/B      | Am
From the bottomless pit.
       G             Em
But my hand was made strong
|C         G/B      | Am
By the hand of the Almighty,
    G              Em
We forward in this generation
 C         D
  Triumphantly.
```

Chorus 1

```
 D          G  |C      D    |G
Won't you help to sing  these songs of freedom?
      |C  D    |Em|C    D    |G
'Cause all I ever had:      redemption songs,
|C   D      |G    |C  D    |
   Redemption songs
```

Verse 2
Emancipate yourselves from mental slavery,
None but ourselves can free our minds.
Have no fear for atomic energy
'Cause none of them can stop the time.
How long shall they kill our prophets
While we stand aside and look?
Some say it's just a part of it,
We've got to fulfill the Book.

Chorus 2 As Chorus 1

Verse 3 As Verse 2

Chorus 2 As Chorus 1

© COPYRIGHT 1980 FIFTY-SIX HOPE ROAD MUSIC LIMITED/ODNIL MUSIC LIMITED.
BLUE MOUNTAIN MUSIC LIMITED.
ALL RIGHTS RESERVED. INTERNATIONAL COPYRIGHT SECURED.

Introduction

Another essential Bob Marley song to learn, initially released on the album *Uprising* in 1979.

Intro Riff

Try playing the intro riff to this song before strumming:

Strumming

The rhythm playing on the original recording of this song is pretty free, and it mixes the pattern shown here with basic continuous eighth-notes. So, it's best to start with this pattern, and then check out the original to listen for variations that you can play.

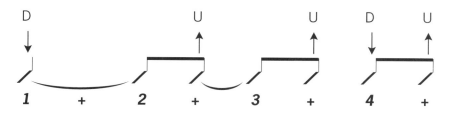

Wonderful Tonight
Words & Music by Eric Clapton

Intro ‖: G | D/F♯ | C | D :‖

Verse 1
G   D/F♯   C   D
It's late in the evening,   she's wondering what clothes to wear.
G   D/F♯   C   D
She puts on her make-up,   and brushes her long blonde hair.
C   D | G   D/F♯ |Em
And then she asks me,   "do I look al - right?"
             C   D   G
And I say, "yes, you look wonderful to - night."

Link | (G) | D/F♯ | C | D |

Verse 2
We go to a party, and everyone turns to see
This beautiful lady, that's walking around with me.
And then she asks me, "Do you feel alright?"
And I say, "Yes, I feel wonderful tonight."

Bridge
     C   D
I feel wonderful be - cause I see
 |G   D/F♯ |Em
The love-light in your eyes,
      C   D
And the wonder of it all
            C   D   (G)
Is that you just don't realise how much I love you.

Link ‖: G | D/F♯ | C | D :‖
(love you.)

Verse 3
It's time to go home now and I've got an aching head,
So I give her the car keys, she helps me to bed.
And then I tell her as I turn out the light,
I say, "My darling, you were wonderful tonight.
Oh, my darling, you were wonderful tonight."

Outro ‖: G | D/F♯ | C | D :‖ G |

© COPYRIGHT 1977, 1999 & 2004 ERIC CLAPTON.
ALL RIGHTS RESERVED. INTERNATIONAL COPYRIGHT SECURED.

Introduction
One of several tributes by Eric Clapton to his lover Pattie Boyd, then George Harrison's wife.

Jammin'
If you have a friend who knows how to play the G major scale, they could try improvising over the chords for this song as you play them, as that scale will work for the entire sequence! We will cover the G major scale in the Intermediate Method.

Finger-Picking Pattern
Once you get the picking pattern right on the G chord you can play the same for all the other chords, but of course the bass will change with the chords. It sounds great once you get it and it's worth working on, even if it's pretty tricky at first: it will really help you pick accurately.

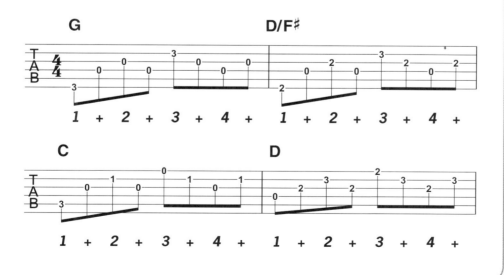

The A Team
Words & Music by Ed Sheeran

Capo Fret 2

Verse 1
```
        G         G       G              |G   D/F#   |Em
    White lips, pale face, breathing in   snowflakes,
          C             G     G
    Burnt lungs, sour taste.
    G         G       G            |G    D/F#  |Em
    Light's gone, day's end, struggl - ing to pay  rent,
          C              G    G
    Long nights, strange men.
```

Chorus 1
```
           Am7              Am7         C
    And they say she's in the class A team,
    C         G              G             D/F#
    Stuck in her daydream, been this way since eighteen.
         D/F#     Am7           Am7              C
    But lately her face seems slowly sinking, wasting,
        C            G         G
    Crumbling like pastries, and they scream
         D/F#                      D/F#
    The worst things in life come free to us.
          Em                  C
    Cause we're just under the upper hand
      G                   G
       And go mad for a couple grams,
    Em              C             G      G
    And she don't want to go outside    tonight.
             Em                     C
    And in a pipe she flies to the Motherland
       G                 G
       Or sells love to another man.
    Em          C      G    D/F#    Em  C  G G           Em C G G
      It's too cold   outside   for angels to fly,      angels to fly.
```

Verse 2
Ripped gloves, raincoat, tried to swim and stay afloat,
Dry house, wet clothes.
Loose change, bank notes, weary-eyed, dry throat,
Call girl, no phone.

Chorus 2 As Chorus 1

Bridge
```
          D/F#      Am7        Am7         C    C         Em
    (...for angels to fly), That angel will die covered in white,
    Em             G                    G
    Closed eye and hoping for a better life.
    Am7       Am7              C          C                    (Em)
    This time,   we'll fade out tonight, straight down the line.
```

Instr.
```
||: Em   | C    | G    | G    :||
```

Chorus 3 As Chorus 1 *(Repeat)*

© COPYRIGHT 2010 SONY/ATV MUSIC PUBLISHING.
ALL RIGHTS RESERVED. INTERNATIONAL COPYRIGHT SECURED.

Introduction

A singer-songwriter with a social conscience, Ed Sheeran wrote this song when he was just 18 years old, after playing a gig at a homeless shelter.

Little Finger Variation

I love this song and it's great to see a young guy coming up, writing his own songs, and playing hundreds of gigs to hone his craft. There is an amazing version of him playing this song solo on a canal boat which you should look up, and see how he uses dynamics (loud and soft) and slight changes to the strumming pattern to keep the performance interesting. He's also using a nice chord grip by placing his little finger on the 3rd fret of the thinnest string for the Am (to make it an Am7) and leaving it down for the C chord which sounds lovely.

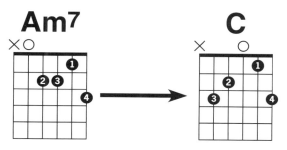

Strumming

Ed Sheeran strums this song without a pick, using mainly his thumb for the down-strums on beats 1 and 3 and his first finger for the rest. The most noticeable thing is the strong accent on beats 2 and 4—a 'muted hit', which we will cover in the Intermediate Course—but which you can achieve now by playing those beats a little harder. Don't feel you have to stick with his way of doing it. You may want to simplify it, especially if you want to sing at the same time. There are many other patterns we have covered in this course that will work (even 'Old Faithful'), so it's best if you experiment and see which ones work for you.

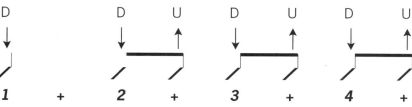

Zombie
Words & Music by Dolores O'Riordan

Chord progression throughout:

| Em | Cmaj7 | G6 | G6/F# |

Verse 1

Another head hangs lowly, child is slowly taken.
And the violence caused such silence, who are we mistaken?
But you see, it's not me, it's not my family,
In your head, in your head, they are fighting.
With their tanks and their bombs
And their bombs and their guns,
in your head, in your head they are crying.

Chorus 1

In your head, in your head,
Zombie, zombie, zombie, hey, hey.
What's in your head, in your head?
Zombie, zombie, zombie, hey, hey, hey.

Bridge 1

Oh, doo, doo, doo, doo…

Verse 2

Another mother's breakin' heart
Is taking over.
When the violence causes silence,
We must be mistaken.
It's the same old theme
Since nineteen sixteen,
In your head, in your head,
They're still fighting.
With their tanks and their bombs
And their bombs and their guns,
In your head, in your head they are dying.

Chorus 2   As Chorus 1

Bridge 2   As Bridge 1

© COPYRIGHT 1994 ISLAND MUSIC LIMITED.
UNIVERSAL/ISLAND MUSIC LIMITED.
ALL RIGHTS RESERVED. INTERNATIONAL COPYRIGHT SECURED.

Introduction

The Cranberries' 1994 protest song.

Playing with Two Guitars

If you have a friend to play with, this song is a great one to have fun playing two different parts together. One plays the kind of heavy parts and one plays the clean. In the verses, one strums and one picks out random notes one at a time; in the chorus one plays the heavy eighth-notes (just using down-strums), and the other plays the strum pattern shown below.

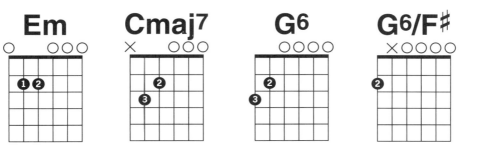

Strumming

This part is the clean strumming part like you hear right at the start of the song. The heavy part just plays all down-strums.

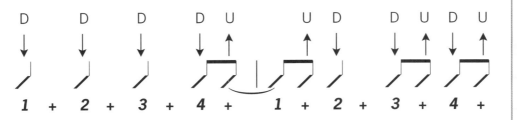

Hand In My Pocket
Words by Alanis Morissette • Music by Alanis Morissette & Glen Ballard

Verse 1

G^5 (8 bars)
I'm broke but I'm happy, I'm poor but I'm kind,
I'm short but I'm healthy, yeah.
I'm high but I'm grounded, I'm sane but I'm overwhelmed,
I'm lost but I'm hopeful baby.

Chorus 1

                         G^5/F $Csus^2$
And what it all comes down to
                              G^5 G^5
Is that everything's gonna be fine, fine, fine,
        G^5/F
'Cause I got one hand in my pocket
| $Csus^2$ G^5/D | G^5
And the other one is giving a high five.

Verse 2

I feel drunk but I'm sober, I'm young and I'm underpaid,
I'm tired but I'm working, yeah.
I care but I'm restless, I'm here but I'm really gone,
I'm wrong and I'm sorry baby.

Chorus 2

And what it all comes down to
Is that everything's gonna be quite alright,
'Cause I've got one hand in my pocket
And the other one is flicking a cigarette.

Chorus 3

And what it all comes down to
Is that I haven't got it all figured out just yet,
'Cause I've got one hand in my pocket
And the other one is giving a peace sign.

Verse 3

I'm free but I'm focused, I'm green but I'm wise,
I'm hard but I'm friendly baby.
I'm sad but I'm laughing, I'm brave but I'm chicken shit,
I'm sick but I'm pretty baby.

Chorus 4

And what it all boils down to
Is that no one's really got it figured out just yet.
But I've got one hand in my pocket
And the other one is playing a piano.
And what it all comes down to my friends
Is that every thing is just fine, fine, fine,
'Cause I've got one hand in my pocket
And the other one is hailing a taxi cab.

© COPYRIGHT 1995 MUSIC CORPORATION OF AMERICA INCORPORATED/VANHURST
PLACEMUSIC/MCA MUSIC PUBLISHING/AEROSTATION CORPORATION, USA.
UNIVERSAL/MCA MUSIC LIMITED.
ALL RIGHTS RESERVED. INTERNATIONAL COPYRIGHT SECURED.

Introduction

This was one of several massive singles from Alanis Morrisette's *Jagged Little Pill* album (released in 1995), alongside 'You Oughta Know' and 'Ironic'.

Holding down notes

This song uses the trick of holding down a couple of notes through all the chords for the whole song. Your 3rd and 4th fingers will hold down the thinnest two strings at the 3rd fret for the whole thing. Just the bass note moves around! You play the G and C bass notes with your 2nd finger and the F with your 1st finger, which might seem a stretch at first but you'll soon be used to it.

G5    **G5/F**    **Csus2**    **G5/D**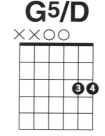

Strumming

There are many guitar layers in this song, but this song will sound great with this simplified pattern.

D	D	D U	D
		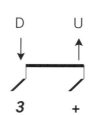	
1 +	2 +	3 +	4 +

Let It Be

Words & Music by John Lennon & Paul McCartney

Intro
| C G | Am Fmaj7 | C G | F C |

Verse 1
       |C   G
When I find myself in times of trouble,
Am   Fmaj7|
Mother Mary comes to me,
C   G |F C
Speaking words of wisdom, let it be.
   |C   G
And in my hour of darkness
   |Am   Fmaj7 |
She is standing right in front of me,
C   G |F C
Speaking words of wisdom, let it be.

Chorus 1
   |Am   C/G |F   C |
Let it be, let it be, let it be, let it be,
C   G |F C |
Whisper words of wisdom, let it be.

Verse 2
And when the broken-hearted people
Living in the world agree,
There will be an answer, let it be.
For though they may be parted there is
Still a chance that they will see.
There will be an answer, let it be.

Chorus 2
Let it be, let it be, let it be, let it be,
There will be an answer, let it be.
Let it be, let it be, let it be, let it be,
Whisper words of wisdom, let it be.

Link
| F C | G F C | F C | G F C |

Solo
‖: C G | Am F | C G | F C :‖

Chorus 3
As Chorus 1

Verse 3
And when the night is cloudy,
There is still a light that shines on me,
Shine until tomorrow, let it be.
I wake up to the sound of music,
Mother Mary comes to me,
Speaking words of wisdom, let it be.

Chorus 4
As Chorus 1

© COPYRIGHT 1970 SONY/ATV MUSIC PUBLISHING.
ALL RIGHTS RESERVED. INTERNATIONAL COPYRIGHT SECURED.

BONUS SONGS

 ### Introduction

Now we are just consolidating what you (hopefully!) already know. Well done on making it this far, I really hope you are feeling confident with it all. If not, now is the time to go and revise the things that you are struggling with. My advice is to pick songs that you found hard and work them until you get it right. You will find that perfecting one song will help you play many of the other songs, because the skills you've learnt are likely to come up several times in other songs.

There are some super-cool tunes in this bonus stage. Some are a bit tricky, but you're are up for a challenge, aren't you?

 ### Bonus songs: Your notes

You're Beautiful

Words & Music by Sacha Skarbek, James Blunt & Amanda Ghost

Capo Fret 8

Verse 1

        G   G/F#
My life is brilliant,   my love is pure,
   Em7   Cadd9
  I saw an angel   of that I'm sure.
           G   G/F#
She smiled at me on the subway, she was with another man.
       Em7   Em7
But I won't lose no sleep on that, 'cause I've got a plan.

Chorus 1

|Cadd9   Dsus4 |G
  You're beauti - ful,   you're beautiful,
|Cadd9   Dsus4 |G
  You're beauti - ful, it's true.
| Cadd9   Dsus4 |G   G/F# | Em7
I saw your face   in a crowd - ed   place
|Cadd9   D |Em7
And I don't know what to do,
|Cadd9   D |G
'Cause I'll never be   with you.

Link 1

| (G) | G/F# | Em7 | Cadd9 |

Verse 2

Yeah, she caught my eye as I walked on by
She could see from my face that I was flying high.
And I don't think that I'll see her again,
But we shared a moment that will last till the end.

Chorus 2

As Chorus 1

Bridge

|Cadd9   Em7 |
  La la la   la
|Cadd9   Em7 |
  La la la   la
|Cadd9   Em7 |Am D |
  La la la   la la

Chorus 3

You're beautiful, you're beautiful,
You're beautiful, it's true.
There must be an angel with a smile on her face
            |Cadd9   Dsus4 |G G/F# |Em7   Em7
When she thought up that I should be with you.
But it's time to face the truth,
I will never be with you.

© COPYRIGHT 2004 EMI MUSIC PUBLISHING LIMITED (63%)/BUCKS MUSIC GROUP LIMITED (37%).
ALL RIGHTS RESERVED. INTERNATIONAL COPYRIGHT SECURED.

Introduction

James Blunt's breakthrough single from 2005.

Quick change

Watch out for the quick chord change in the chorus—there's a sneaky 2/4 bar for the change from G to G/F# ('crowd - ed'). The chord shapes for this song keep the 3rd and 4th fingers down on the 3rd fret of the top two strings for most of the song:

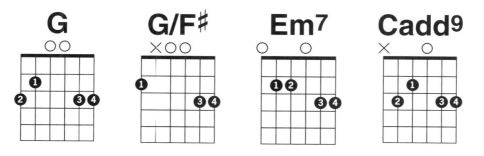

Strumming

The strumming in this tune is really in sixteenth-notes, but I've written it as eighth-notes so you will understand it. It will sound the same. Remember to play it real slow to get it right and then speed it up—and don't be afraid to count along if it helps.

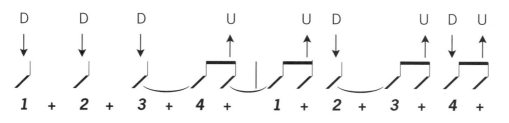

Imagine
Words & Music by John Lennon

Intro

| C Cmaj7 | F | C Cmaj7 | F |

Verse 1

C   Cmaj7 |F |
Imagine there's no heaven,
C   Cmaj7 |F |
It's easy if you   try.
C   Cmaj7 |F |
No hell below   us,
C   Cmaj7 |F |
Above us only   sky.
F   C/E |Dm   Dm/C |
Imagine all the people
G   C |G7 |
Living for to - day.

Verse 2

Imagine there's no countries,
It isn't hard to do.
Nothing to kill or die for,
And no religion too.
Imagine all the people
Living life in peace.

Chorus 1

|F   G |C   Cmaj7 E E7 |
 You may say I'm a dreamer,
|F   G |C Cmaj7 E E7 |
 But I'm not the only one.
|F   G |C   Cmaj7 E E7 |
 I hope some day you'll join us,
|F   G |C |
 And the world will be as one.

Verse 3

Imagine no possessions,
I wonder if you can.
No need for greed or hunger,
A brotherhood of man.
Imagine all the people
Sharing all the world.

Chorus 2

As Chorus 1

© COPYRIGHT 1971 LENONO MUSIC.
ALL RIGHTS RESERVED. INTERNATIONAL COPYRIGHT SECURED.

Introduction

John Lennon's plea for peace, first released on the album of the same name in 1971.

Melodic Chords

In the chorus there is a really nice chord progression—C, Cmaj7, E, E7. Start with C and then lift your 1st finger off to get Cmaj7; then change to E; then add you little finger to the 3rd fret of the second string to get the E7. It's like a little countermelody and adding things like that really make your playing sound cool.

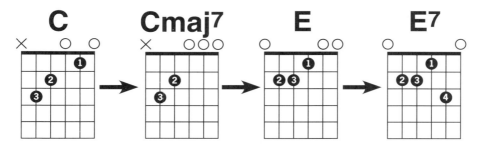

Also, watch out for these new slash chords near the end of each verse:

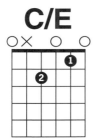
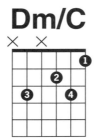

 Strumming

This is a piano song, so you really can try out strumming whatever patterns you like. Watch out for the placement of the chord changes: the Cmaj7 chord, for instance, appears on beat 4.

Hey, Soul Sister

Words & Music by Espen Lind, Patrick Monahan & Amund Bjoerklund

Capo Fret 4

Verse 1
```
        C              G                    Am            F
Your lipstick stains    on the front lobe of my left-side brains.
                        C
I knew I wouldn't for - get you
                G                    Am      |F  G |
And so I went and let you blow my mind.
        C              G
Your sweet moon beam,
                        Am            F
The smell of you in every single dream I dream.
                        C
I knew when we col - lided,
                G                    Am      |F  G |
You're the one I have de - cided who's one of my kind.
```

Chorus 1
```
F         |G           C    G    |F
Hey soul sister, ain't that Mr. Mister on the radio, stereo,
 |G                   C    G    |
The way you move ain't fair, you know.
F         |G           C    G    |F         G   C
Hey soul sister, I  don't want to miss a single thing you do__ to - night.
         G     Am         F
Hey,___ hey,___ hey.___
```

Verse 2
Just in time, I'm so glad you have a one-track mind like me.
You gave my life direction,
A game show love connection we can't deny, ay, ay.
I'm so obsessed,
My heart is bound to beat right out my untrimmed chest.
I believe in you, like a virgin, you're Madonna,
And I'm always gonna wanna blow your mind.

Chorus 2   As Chorus 1

Bridge
```
        C                    G                        Am
The way you can cut a rug,    watching you's the only drug I need.
                                   F
You're so gangsta, I'm so thug, you're the only one I'm dreaming of.
            C                         G
You see, I can be myself now final - ly,
                                Am
In fact there's nothing I can't be.
            Am           |F    G   |
I want the world to see you be with     me.
```

Chorus 3   As Chorus 1

© COPYRIGHT 2009 BLUE LAMP MUSIC/EMI APRIL MUSIC INCORPORATED, USA/STELLAR SONGS LIMITED.
EMI MUSIC PUBLISHING LIMITED.
ALL RIGHTS RESERVED. INTERNATIONAL COPYRIGHT SECURED.

Introduction

The original recording of this features ukulele, but it sounds great on a guitar with a capo as well!

Chord changes

The number of beats and bars that you play each chord for in this song varies quite a bit—so you'll have to get your ear working to make sure you do the right number of strums per chord. Listen carefully to the original record, follow the vocal melody, and you'll get there.

Strumming

This basic pattern is pretty consistent but you can add a little up-strum on the 'and' after 4 sometimes too if you like!

D		D	U	D	U	D	U
1	+	2	+	3	+	4	+

Wild World
Words & Music by Cat Stevens

Intro

| Am   D/F♯ | G
La la la la, la la la la la, la
          C | F
La la la la, la la la la la, la
          Dm | E   Esus⁴ |
La la la la, la la la la la, la la.

Verse 1

| Am   D/F♯ | G
Now that I've lost everything to you,
          C | F
You say you wanna start something new
          Dm | E
And it's breakin' my heart you're leavin',
          Esus⁴ |
Baby, I'm grievin'.
| Am   D/F♯ | G
But if you wanna leave, take good care,
          C | F
I hope you have a lot of nice things to wear,
          Dm | E | G   G⁷ G⁶ G |
But then a lot of nice things turn bad out there.

Chorus 1

  C   G | F
Oh, baby, baby, it's a wild world,
| G   F | C   G |
It's hard to get by just upon a smile.
  C   G | F
Oh, baby, baby, it's a wild world,
| G   F | C   Dm   E |
I'll always remember you like a child, girl.

Verse 2

You know I've seen a lot of what the world can do
And it's breakin' my heart in two
Because I never wanna see you a sad girl,
Don't be a bad girl.
But if you wanna leave, take good care,
I hope you make a lot of nice friends out there,
But just remember there's a lot of bad and beware.

Chorus 2

As Chorus 1

Solo

| Am | D/F♯ | G |
          C   F
La la la la, la la la la la, la
          Dm   E
La la la la, la la la la la la, la la.

© COPYRIGHT 1970 SALAFA LIMITED.
ALL RIGHTS RESERVED. INTERNATIONAL COPYRIGHT SECURED.

Verse 3
Baby, I love you,
But if you wanna leave, take good care,
I hope you make a lot of nice friends out there,
But just remember there's a lot of bad and beware.

Chorus 3
As Chorus 1

Chorus 4
Oh, baby, baby, it's a wild world,
And it's hard to get by just upon a smile.
Oh, baby, baby, it's a wild world,
And I'll always remember you like a child, girl.

Introduction
This was a hit for Cat Stevens in 1970, from his classic album *Tea For The Tillerman*.

The 'G' Walk-down

At the end of the verse you get a little G, G7, G6, G thing going on which is a little melodic idea you can add into your rhythm playing. Start with a regular G chord using three fingers (easiest is the folk shape using fingers 2, 3 and 4); to play the G7 you will take off your little finger and add your 1st finger on the 1st fret on the thinnest string. Then to get the G6 you would remove your 1st finger too (so all the four thinnest strings would be open) and then finally to get the next G, you would use the 'Big' G (the one that uses all four fingers) but don't play the thinnest string, so the highest note you play will be the note D.

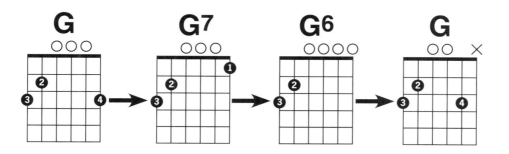

Watch out for the quick change from E to these chords at the end of the verse—this is a 2/4 bar.

Use Somebody

Words & Music by Caleb Followill, Nathan Followill, Jared Followill & Matthew Followill

Intro

‖: C5 | C/E | F5 | F5 :‖

‖: A5 | C5 | F5 | F5 :‖

Verse 1

(F)   C5   C/E   F5   F5
I've been roaming a - round always looking down at all I see.

         C5   C/E   F5   F5
Painted faces fill the places I can't reach.

                   A5   C5 F5 F5
‖: You know that I could use somebody, :‖

Verse 2

Someone like you and all you know and how you speak.
Countless lovers undercover of the street.
You know that I could use somebody (x2)
You know that I could use somebody,
Someone like you.

Link

As Intro

Verse 3

Off in the night, while you live it up I'm off to sleep.
Waging wars to shake the poet and the beat.
I hope it's gonna make you notice (x2)
Someone like me, (x3)
Somebody.

Bridge

D5   D5   F#5
   Go and let it out, go and let it out,

  F#5   D5
Go and let it out, go and let it out,

    D5   F#5
Go and let it out, go and let it out,

   B5
Go and let it out, go and let it out.

Outro

| C5 | C/E | F5 | F5 |

| A5 | C5 | F5 |

F5   A5   C5 F5
‖: Someone like you,   somebody. :‖ *Play x3*

             C5   C/E   F5
I've been roaming a - round, always lookin' down at all I see.

© COPYRIGHT 2008 FOLLOWILL MUSIC/MARTHA STREET MUSIC/SONGS OF COMBUSTION
(ADMINSTERED BY BUG MUSIC-MUSIC OF WINDSWEPT) (55%)/MCFEARLESS MUSIC/COFFEE
TEA OR ME PUBLISHING (ADMINSTERED BY BUG MUSIC LIMITED) (45%).
ALL RIGHTS RESERVED. INTERNATIONAL COPYRIGHT SECURED.

Introduction

This song was one of the singles from Kings Of Leon's 2008 album *Only By The Night*, which saw the band rise to become one of the biggest in the world.

 ## Chords

Play power chords in the bridge of this song; here are the chord shapes for the Intro and Verses etc:

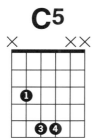

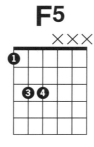
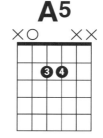

Strumming

This song should be played using all down-strums. To get it to sound just like the record, it is important to catch the accent patterns. They change a lot through the song, so it's not like there is a set one; the best thing is to listen a bunch of times and get the sound in your head. This is really important. Again, if you don't really know what it should sound like there is little chance of you getting it right!

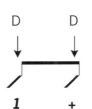
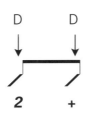
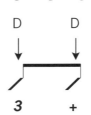
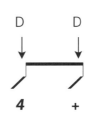

Stuck In The Middle With You
Words & Music by Gerry Rafferty & Joe Egan

Intro

| D | D | D | D |

Verse 1

      D   D
Well I don't know why I came here tonight,
      D   D
I got the feeling that something ain't   right.
      G⁷   G⁷
I'm so scared in case I fall off my chair
      D   D
And I'm wondering how I'll get down those stairs.
  A⁷ | C   G⁷
Clowns to the left of me, jokers to the right.
| D   D
Here I am, stuck in the middle with you.

Verse 2

Yes I'm stuck in the middle with you
And I'm wondering what it is I should do.
It's so hard to keep the smile from my face,
Losing control, yeah I'm all over the place.
Clowns to the left of me, jokers to the right.
Here I am, stuck in the middle with you.

Middle 1

        G⁷
Well, you started out with nothing
        G⁷   D   D
And you're proud that you're a self-made man,
        G⁷
And your friends they all come crawling,
G⁷   D   D   Am   Am
Slap you on the back and say "Please,___   please."

Link 1

| D | D | D | D |

Verse 3

Well I'm trying to make some sense of it all
But I can see that it makes no sense at all.
Is it cool to go to sleep on the floor?
I don't think that I can take anymore.
Clowns to the left of me, jokers to the right.
Here I am, stuck in the middle with you.

Instrumental

As Verse chords

© COPYRIGHT 1972 STAGE THREE MUSIC (CATALOGUES) LTD ADMINISTERED BY STAGE THREE MUSIC PUBLISHING LTD)/
BABY BUN MUSIC LIMITED.
ALL RIGHTS RESERVED. INTERNATIONAL COPYRIGHT SECURED.

Middle 2	As Middle 1
Link 2	As Link 1
Verse 4	As verse 1
Outro	Guess I'm D stuck in the middle with you, D D Stuck in the middle with you, D D D Here I am stuck in the middle with you.

Introduction

Now associated with an infamous scene in Quentin Tarantino's film *Reservoir Dogs*, this was originally a hit for Stealers Wheel in 1972.

Percussive strums

On beats 2 and 4 of this song there is a percussive strum. It's the kind of strumming trick that sounds really cool, but can be pretty hard for a beginner. That said, if you are feeling confident with your strumming thus far, then you might like to use your percussive hit on beats 2 and 4 in this song—it will sound awesome!

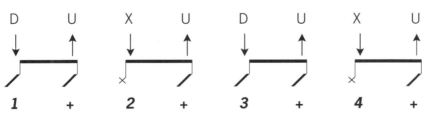

Dream Catch Me

Words & Music by Crispin Hunt, Newton Faulkner & Gordon Mills

Capo Fret 7

Verse 1

   G/B G/B   Csus²   Csus²   G/B G/B   Csus²   Csus²
Eve - ry time   I close my eyes,
  Am Am   C   C   G   G   Em
It's you   and I know now   who I am.
Em   Am   Am
Yeah, yeah, yeah,
     D   D
And I know now.

Pre-chorus 1

G   G   D
There's a place I go when I'm a - lone,
        D   Em
Do anything I want, be anyone I wanna be.
      Em   C   C
But it is us I see and I cannot be - lieve I'm falling.
G   G   D
That's where I'm going, where are you go - ing?
   D   Em
Hold it close, won't let this go.

Chorus 1

   Em   Cmaj7
Dream catch me, yeah,
   Cmaj7   Am   Cmaj7
Dream catch me when I fall,
                   G/B
Or else I won't come back at all.

Verse 2

You do so much that you don't know,
It's true and I know now who I am.
Yeah, yeah, yeah,
And I know now.

Pre-chorus 2   As Pre-chorus 1

Chorus 2   As Chorus 1

Bridge

Em   C   G
See you as a mountain, a fountain of God,
          D   Em
See you as a descant soul in the setting sun.
         C   G
Nuance of sound has decided it's love,
 D   D
I'm young.

© COPYRIGHT 2007 BLUE SKY MUSIC LIMITED/SONY/ATV MUSIC PUBLISHING (45%)/
NBF MUSIC PUBLISHING LIMITED/PEERMUSIC (UK) LIMITED (35%)/
OUTCASTE MUSIC PUBLISHING LIMITED (20%).
ALL RIGHTS RESERVED. INTERNATIONAL COPYRIGHT SECURED.

Pre-chorus 3   There's a place I go when I'm alone,
Do anything I want, be anyone I wanna be.
But it is us I see and I cannot believe I'm falling.

Pre-chorus 4   As Pre-chorus 1

Chorus 3
    Em   **Em**   **Cmaj7**
Dream catch me, yeah,
     Cmaj7   **Am** **Cmaj7**
Dream catch me when I fall,
                      G
Or else I won't come back at all.

Introduction
Newton Faulkner is famed for his incredible acoustic style, using percussive techniques, tapping and harmonics, but fortunately for us he stuck to simple strumming on this 2007 hit.

Chords

Keep your 3rd and 4th fingers on the thinnest two strings at the 3rd fret for the chord shapes in the verses:

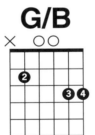
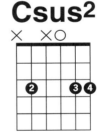

Strumming Dynamics

The strumming in this song is relentless eighth-note down-strums so you MUST explore the dynamics to make it sound cool. As well as making the verses quieter, try playing just the thicker bass strings in the verses and then playing the full chord for the choruses.

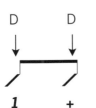

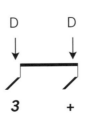
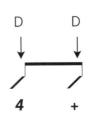

Substitute
Words & Music by Pete Townshend

Verse 1

```
D           G              D        D
You think we look pretty good to - gether,
D           G              D        D
You think my shoes are made of leather.
```

Pre-chorus 1

```
         Em                 Em
But I'm a substitute for a - nother guy,
     Em              Em
I look pretty tall but my heels are high.
       Em                Em
The simple things you see are all complicated.
     Em                 Em        | A   Asus4 | A
I look pretty young but I'm just backdated, yeah.
```

Chorus 1

(with main riff)
(Sub - sti - tute) lies for the fact:
I see right through your plastic mac.
I look all white but my Dad was black.
My fine-looking suit is really made out of sack.

Verse 2

I was born with a plastic spoon in my mouth,
North side of my town faced east and the east was facing south.

Pre-chorus 2

And now you dare to look me in the eye
But crocodile tears are what you cry.
If it's a genuine problem you won't try
To work it out at all, just pass it by,
Pass it by.

Chorus 2

(with main riff)
(Sub - sti - tute) me for him,
(Sub - sti - tute) my Coke for gin.
(Sub - sti - tute) you for my Mum,
At least I'll get my washing done.

Solo

‖: D | G | D | D :‖

Pre-chorus 3 As Pre-chorus 1

Link (main riff x4)

Verse 3 As Verse 2

Pre-chorus 4 As Pre-chorus 1

Chorus 3 As Chorus 2

Chorus 4 As Chorus 1

© COPYRIGHT 1966 FABULOUS MUSIC LIMITED.
ALL RIGHTS RESERVED. INTERNATIONAL COPYRIGHT SECURED.

Introduction

One of The Who's early hits, from 1966.

Triads

This song uses triad shapes in the chorus riff, which is the main riff of the song. Triads are really fun to play about with (and covered in the Intermediate Method Foundation if you want to sneak a look now) for making riffs, as in this song, but also they sound great as a second guitar part if you want to jam along with another guitar player.

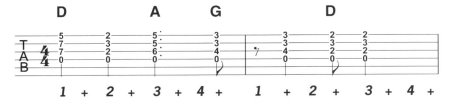

More Riffs

The verse and pre-chorus can be strummed using 'Old Faithful', but the recording uses specific riffs. The verse riff is played using a D chord, lifting the first finger to play the note on the 5th string.

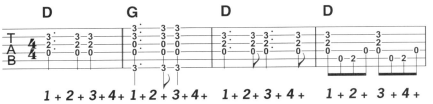

The pre-chorus riff is tricky to sing along with, but great fun to play. If you want to sing along, I'd recommend just strumming the chord.

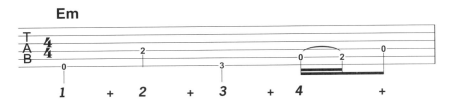

Driftwood
Words & Music by Fran Healy

Capo Fret 7

Verse 1

    D   G⁶ |Asus⁴   A |
Everything is open, nothing is set in stone
    D   G⁶ |Asus⁴   A |
Rivers turn to oceans, oceans tide you home
    D   G⁶ |Asus⁴   A |
Home is where the heart is, but your heart had to roam
    D   G⁶ |Asus⁴   A |
Drifting over bridges, never to return
    A⁷
Watching bridges burn.

Chorus 1

    |D   A |Em
You're driftwood floating under - water
            G⁶   G⁶
Breaking into pieces, pieces, pieces
   |D   A |Em
Just driftwood, hollow and of no use
          G⁶   G⁶
Waterfalls will find you, bind you, grind you.

Verse 2

Nobody is an island, everyone has to go
Pillars turn to butter, butterflying low
Low is where your heart is, but your heart has to grow
Drifting under bridges, never with the flow.

Bridge 1

            Em |Asus⁴   A
And you really didn't think it would happen
   |Em |Asus⁴   A
But it really is the end of the line
   |D   A |Em
So I'm sorry   that you've turned to driftwood
             G⁶   D
But you've been drifting for a long, long time.

Interlude

|Em |Asus⁴ A |Em |Asus⁴ A |Em |Asus⁴ A |Em |Em |

Verse 3

Everywhere there's trouble, nowhere's safe to go
Pushes turn to shovels, shovelling the snow
Frozen you have chosen, the path you wish to go
Drifting now forever, and forever more
Until you reach your shore.

Chorus 2   As Chorus 1

Bridge 2   As Bridge 1

Outro

You've been drifting, for a long, long time
You've been drifting for a long, long
Drifting for a long, long time.

© COPYRIGHT 1999 SONY/ATV MUSIC PUBLISHING.
ALL RIGHTS RESERVED. INTERNATIONAL COPYRIGHT SECURED.

Introduction

This song featured on the Travis album *The Man Who*, which was a massive success in 1999.

G6

The G6 chord used here is like the 'Big' G using all four fingers but with the little finger removed so that the thin E string is open. This makes the change to D and Asus4 very easy and gives the verses a cool character!

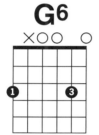

Strumming

This song uses consistent strumming; it's really using accents that give the groove. So strum evenly up and down four times in each beat (a nice introduction to sixteenth-note strumming!) and then start just putting an accent on the beat each time. It sounds great and as you get better you can experiment with moving the accents and making the grooves more complex.

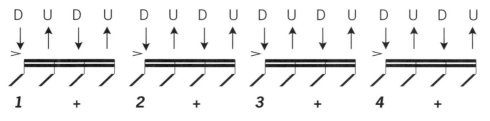

Times Like These

Words & Music by Dave Grohl, Taylor Hawkins, Nate Mendel & Chris Shiflett

Intro

‖: D⁷add⁶ | D⁷add⁶ | D⁷add⁶ | D⁷add⁶ :‖

Instrumental

7/4 | D5 | C5 | B5 | D |
| C5 | B5 | D | C5 |
4/4 | B5 | B5 | D⁷add⁶ | D⁷add⁶ | D⁷add⁶ | D⁷add⁶ |

Verse 1

```
D  D              Am7      Am7
I,    I'm a one-way motorway,
                  C           Em          D7add6   D7add6
I'm the one that drives away, follows you back home
D  D              Am7      Am7
I,    I'm a street light shining,
                  C              Em         D7add6   D7add6
I'm a white light blinding bright, burning off and on.
             D7add6   D7add6
Uh - huh - uh.
```

Chorus 1

```
        C           Em           D
It's times like these you learn to live a - gain,
        C           Em           D
It's times like these you give, and give a - gain,
        C           Em           D
It's times like these you learn to love a - gain,
        C           Em         D7add6  D7add6  D7add6  D7add6
It's times like these, time and time a - gain.
```

Verse 2

I, I'm a new day rising,
I'm a brand new sky to hang the stars upon to - night.
I, I'm a little divided,
Do I stay or run away and leave it all be - hind?
Uh - huh - uh

Chorus 2   As Chorus 1

Instr. 2   As Instrumental chords

Chorus 3

```
          C           Em           D
‖: It's times like these you learn to live a - gain,
          C           Em           D
   It's times like these you give, and give a - gain,
          C           Em           D
   It's times like these you learn to love a - gain,
          C           Em           D
   It's times like these, time and time a - gain. :‖
```

© COPYRIGHT 2002 M.J.-TWELVE MUSIC/FLYING EARFORM MUSIC/EMI VIRGIN SONGS
INCORPORATED/LIVING UNDER A ROCK MUSIC/I LOVE THE PUNK ROCK MUSIC, USA.
EMI VIRGIN MUSIC LIMITED (75%)/UNIVERSAL/MCA MUSIC LIMITED (25%)
ALL RIGHTS RESERVED. INTERNATIONAL COPYRIGHT SECURED.

Introduction

This song was released on the fourth Foo Fighters album, *One By One*, and can also be heard on their acoustic live album *Skin And Bones*.

 Odd Timings

There is a section of this song in 7/4 time, which means there are seven beats in the bar rather than the usual four. This is pretty tricky for a beginner guitar player, and so my advice is to simply leave it out and play the rest of the song. This tune sounds great on acoustic and will always go down well at a party!

Intro chord

The intro chord is a very interesting one, I've not ever seen it in any other song! Getting the strumming right is the key thing: once you get that, you will be fine with it. Make sure that you mute the thickest string with your thumb and the tip of your second finger. Note that when Dave Grohl plays it live on acoustic he does not play the D7add6 from the record but just plays a regular D chord, and lifts his 1st finger on and off! So you can try playing it that way too if you like.

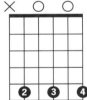

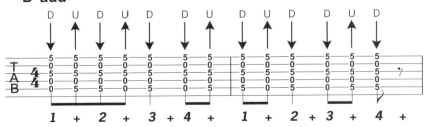

Order No. AM1011538
ISBN: 978-1-4950-6017-5
This book © Copyright 2015 Wise Publications,
a division of Music Sales Limited.

Unauthorised reproduction of any part of this
publication by any means including photocopying
is an infringement of copyright.

Written, compiled and arranged by Justin Sandercoe.
Edited by Tom Farncombe and Toby Knowles.
Design by Fresh Lemon.
Cover design by Paul Agar.
Cover photographs by Nick Delaney.

Your Guarantee of Quality
As publishers, we strive to produce every
book to the highest commercial standards.
This book has been carefully designed to
minimise awkward page turns and to make
playing from it a real pleasure.
Particular care has been given to specifying
acid-free, neutral-sized paper made from pulps
which have not been elemental chlorine bleached.
This pulp is from farmed sustainable forests and was
produced with special regard for the environment.
Throughout, the printing and binding have been
planned to ensure a sturdy, attractive publication
which should give years of enjoyment.
If your copy fails to meet our high standards,
please inform us and we will gladly replace it.